Additional Praise for *Super Sectors*

"John Nyaradi's *Super Sectors* is that rare book that can give anyone—from a relative newcomer right up to the most expert reader—insights into actionable ways to profit from the information presented. From the psychology of investing, to 'point and figure charting' and 'moving average crossovers,' John shows how trading ETFs with sector rotation can beat the pants off 'buy and hold'. He clearly illustrates why his theories have worked in the past and makes a good case for why they'll continue to work in the 'new normal' environment since the 2008 market melt-down. His concluding segment on the Super Sectors he sees dominating future returns should contribute mightily to your future financial well being while letting you feel confident that you're well positioned for what's over today's investment horizon."

> —**Dr. Paul Price**, Founder/Editor, www.BeatingBuffett.com

"If the first decade of the twenty-first century has proved anything, it is that investors cannot afford to let precious time slip through their investment fingers with a buy and hold strategy. Change is occurring too rapidly and trends shift with ever-greater frequency, rendering buy and hold as a high risk strategy unfit for the times. *Super Sectors* goes right to the heart of this issue and provides investors with the vital tools (and reasoning) that will enable them to take advantage of the opportunities such change presents and to help avoid its pitfalls. Investors who read this book will not let that most precious of resources—time—slip by."

> —**Vinny Catalano**, CFA, President and Global Investment Strategist, Blue Marble Research; Nonresident Senior Fellow, Information Technology and Innovation Foundation; Former President, New York Society of Security Analysts; Author, *Sectors and Styles*

"For investors concerned about market volatility and global trends, *Super Sectors* demystifies the technical approaches used by professional traders and offers simple techniques to reduce risk, manage a collection of sector ETFs, and keep a portfolio tuned into the strongest trends. John Nyaradi's bonus interviews on the subject of Super Sectors, with more than fifteen investment experts, are also more than worth the price of the book."

> —**Mark Kramer**, Editor, *Confident Investment Strategies*

"This book clearly answered why buy and hold is the most dangerous and damaging piece of advice in Wall Street. It reviews what ETFs are and how they work. If you want to manage your own retirement or trading accounts through ETFs, this book is a must for you. It summarized major and basic sectors, and how to rotate with scientific methods and trading systems. With more and more people involved in their own financial management, I highly recommend the book to all investors."

> —**John Wang**, CEO, AbleSys; Author, *AbleTrend*

Super Sectors

Founded in 1807, John Wiley & Sons is the oldest independent publishing company in the United States. With offices in North America, Europe, Australia and Asia, Wiley is globally committed to developing and marketing print and electronic products and services for our customers' professional and personal knowledge and understanding.

The Wiley Trading series features books by traders who have survived the market's ever-changing temperament and have prospered—some by reinventing systems, others by getting back to basics. Whether a novice trader, professional or somewhere in between, these books will provide the advice and strategies needed to prosper today and well into the future.

For a list of available titles, visit our Web site at www.WileyFinance.com.

Super Sectors

How to Outsmart the Market Using Sector Rotation and ETFs

JOHN NYARADI

WILEY

John Wiley & Sons, Inc.

Published by John Wiley & Sons, Inc., Hoboken, New Jersey.
Published simultaneously in Canada.

For general information on our other products and services or for technical support, please contact our Customer Care Department within the United States at (800) 762-2974, outside the United States at (317) 572-3993 or fax (317) 572-4002.

Wiley also publishes its books in a variety of electronic formats. Some content that appears in print may not be available in electronic books. For more information about Wiley products, visit our web site at www.wiley.com.

Library of Congress Cataloging-in-Publication Data:

Nyaradi, John.
  Super sectors : how to outsmart the market using sector rotation and ETFs / John Nyaradi.
    p. cm. – (Wiley trading ; 468)
  Includes index.
  ISBN 978-0-470-59250-2 (cloth); ISBN 978-0-470-88030-2 (ebk);
  ISBN 978-0-470-88031-9 (ebk); ISBN 978-0-470-88032-6 (ebk)
  1. Exchange traded funds.   2. Stock funds.   3. Portfolio management.   I. Title.
  HG6043.N93 2010
  332.63′27–dc22

                                                2010030440

Printed in the United States of America

10 9 8 7 6 5 4 3 2 1

For Ann, Chris and Dan,
with love

Contents

Preface

T hanks so much for sharing your valuable time with me and my book, *Super Sectors: How to Outsmart the Market Using Sector Rotation and ETFs*.

This book has been designed to help you avoid bear markets and prosper during bull markets by deploying sector rotation techniques using Exchange Traded Funds.

Some of the techniques outlined in this book are so simple that a sixth grader could do them while others are geared towards the professional trader.

Whether you're a novice trader just looking for ways to get started or a seasoned pro, in these pages you're going to be introduced to valuable trading concepts and get detailed insight into trading systems, opportunities and obstacles so that by the time you reach the end, you will be armed with a powerful arsenal to help you successfully trade Exchange Traded Funds using sector rotation techniques.

If you've suffered through the Bear Market of 2008 and feel less financially secure than you did on October 9th, 2007, when the S&P 500 reached its record closing peak of 1565, you're not alone. Since that fateful autumn Tuesday afternoon, trillions of dollars of assets have been lost in global stock markets and much of that money will likely never be recouped by individual investors. If you lost money over the course of the Bear Market of 2008, I'm looking forward to discussing ways that you can potentially avoid losing money during future bear markets.

However, bear markets aren't the only reason, in my opinion, to actively trade your assets and I say this because as bad as this bear market has been, the losses suffered since late 2007 are not the worst part of the news.

Stock market activity over the last ten years has proven that "buy and hold" is a dead concept and it's very likely that going forward over the next ten years, "buy and hold" will continue to be an invalid and ineffective concept. Because over the last ten years, the S&P 500 has generated a negative rate of return and that doesn't even factor in the ravaging effects that inflation has on your portfolio.

So, in this book we'll discuss why Wall Street's "conventional wisdom" may not be effective going forward and we'll take a close look at the tactical portfolio management alternatives that are available to average retail investors and professionals alike.

Through the pages of this book, you'll learn how you can take control of your destiny and your financial future and not rely on market forces to determine the outcome of your investing activity.

You'll get valuable insights into the features and benefits of Exchange Traded Funds and why they're a great choice for today's active markets.

You'll learn about sector trading and how this style of portfolio management can be one of the most successful you can find and we'll discuss various methods of identifying potential "super sectors," the sectors of the market that are outperforming the general indexes.

As the old saying goes, "there's always a bull market somewhere" and through these pages you'll learn techniques for identifying and profiting from these "super sectors."

Trading systems will be discussed in detail, ranging from the most simple for people who don't want to make trading a "job" all the way to the most detailed and complex systems for professionals who monitor the markets on a daily or even minute by minute basis.

Beyond trading systems we'll look at concepts, challenges and conundrums that all active traders face and how to meet those challenges head on and conquer them.

We'll identify five "super sectors" that quite likely will advance far faster and far higher than the general indexes due to several economic and social "mega trends" that lie just ahead. We'll dive into these macro trends and then identify the sectors that will allow you to gain exposure to these "super sectors" over the coming years.

Finally, we'll have the opportunity to listen to "Interviews with the Experts" in which we'll hear from well-known experts in the fields of investing, technical trading, economics and various market sectors, and we'll gain insight into their views about what opportunities and dangers lie ahead for us as investors.

By the time you finish reading this book, you'll have a wide arsenal of weapons to adapt to your own temperament, trading style and lifestyle so you'll be able to design a complete trading program uniquely suited to you.

And this is important because the bottom line in today's post-crash world is that you're on your own.

You are on your own and you need to arm yourself with the knowledge necessary to survive during what could be very difficult days ahead. No longer can you afford to believe that "the market will come back" or that it will keep going up forever. No longer can you believe that "everything will work out" and no longer can you believe in the "conventional wisdom" spouted by Wall Street and in most of the financial media.

The Great Recession of 2008–2009 has changed everything in the investing landscape, and the "mega trends" I'm going to describe could change it even more drastically. It's quite likely that Darwinian principles of natural selection will be in play and only those who will be able to adapt to this new world will survive and prosper.

A successfully-managed tactical trading program can be the most difficult job in the world or the easiest. It can be one of the most lucrative things you could ever do or it could lead you to financial ruin. Many, many people have tried and failed at active trading and the goal of this book is to arm you with the tools that you need to be successful.

It's not an easy path and it's lined with the school of hard knocks. Along the way you will experience setbacks and failures and feel like giving up, probably more than once. But if you can stick with it, if you can become one of the few who can succeed, you will have the ability to protect and grow your net worth if that's your goal or you will possess the tools necessary to make trading a full time career or second career to supplement your retirement or regular income.

If you can be one of the few who can succeed, you can literally become like the ancient alchemists, able to create money literally out of thin air. When you sit down at your computer and enter some numbers on an order screen, only two things can happen. The numbers can get bigger and be painted green or they can get smaller and be painted red.

The goal of *Super Sectors* is to help you find and stay on the difficult and challenging route to green and growing numbers so that you can grow your wealth, achieve your financial goals and meet the challenges of the demanding days ahead.

Finally, I invite you to visit www.SuperSectors.net for more valuable information about sector rotation using Exchange Traded Funds.

There you'll be able to subscribe to a special membership offer from *Wall Street Sector Selector*, my online newsletter covering sector rotation and Exchange Traded Funds, as well as get more in depth research, reports and links to other leading financial web sites and portals.

I wish you all the best in your endeavors and look forward to working with you towards your trading success.

JOHN NYARADI
Publisher
Wall Street Sector Selector
Bend, Oregon
August 2010

Acknowledgments

Writing a book like this is a mammoth task that couldn't possibly be accomplished by one person alone, no matter how talented or energetic the author might be.

Many people helped *Super Sectors* come to fruition and I would particularly like to thank the following individuals for their help, support and invaluable assistance:

Gabriel Wisdom, fellow pilot, Managing Director and Founder of American Money Management, LLC., who made this entire endeavor possible.

My editors at John Wiley and Sons, Laura Walsh and Judy Howarth, for their expert guidance, encouragement and insight.

The financial and investment experts who were so kind to offer their expertise, insights and unique knowledge to make "Ask the Experts" such a valuable portion of this work. These contributors include Larry Conners, Dr. Marc Faber, Keith Fitz-Gerald, Todd Harrison, Gene Inger, Carl Larry, Timothy Lutts, Tom Lydon, John Mauldin, Lawrence McMillan, Paul Merriman, Michael Moore, Robert Prechter, Jim Rogers, Matthew Simmons, Sam Stovall, Cliff Wachtel, Gabriel Wisdom.

And finally, a special thanks to my family; my wife, Ann, and sons Dan and Chris for your understanding and encouragement during all of the hours and days that disappeared so that *Super Sectors* could become a reality.

Super Sectors

PART I

Five Wall Street Fairy Tales and Why the Conventional Wisdom is Flawed

There are many good reasons to actively manage your portfolio but one of the most compelling is to try to avoid the devastating consequences of bear markets.

Bear markets happen more frequently than you might imagine and do devastating and long-lasting damage to investors' portfolios. But it is possible to avoid these downdrafts and later we'll get into trading systems ranging from simple to complex that are designed to do just that.

For decades, Wall Street and the financial media have fed investors a steady diet of investment advice and concepts that have been proven to be devastatingly flawed during the Tech Wreck of 2000–2002 and again during The Great Recession of 2008.

The financial carnage has been well documented in the press with trillions in assets disappearing, maybe forever, as investors followed advice like "buy and hold," "invest for the long term," and "hang on, it will come back."

And the result was no different during The Great Recession of 2008 than it was during the Tech Wreck or the Bear Market of 1982 or any bear market dating back to the Great Depression.

In every case, the average retail investor typically bought at the top and sold at the bottom and watched the stock market devour his or her hard-earned savings. As the old saying goes, "the stock market will make as big a fool out of as many people as possible," or put another way, "the market will do everything it can to separate you from your money."

In this section we're going to take a look at the 5 Wall Street Fairy Tales that I feel are at the root of these problems and how they're a real and present danger to your net worth. You've heard of all of these before but we're going to delve into each one and see why it's a hazard to your net worth.

And the danger isn't past once The Great Recession ends because there will be other bear markets and other dangers and challenges along our paths.

So let's start with a look at bear markets and how they're an ever-present danger to your portfolio and financial future.

CHAPTER 1

The Bear Facts about Bear Markets

B ear markets are a frequent, normal part of the stock market life cycle, just like recessions are a normal part of the economic cycle and both of these facts create a potentially very dangerous environment for investors around the world.

THE BEAR FACTS: ANOTHER BEAR IS OUT THERE WAITING TO MAUL YOUR PORTFOLIO

Bear markets are defined as drops of 20 percent or more in the overall market typically as defined by the S&P 500, the 500 most widely held stocks in the United States.

Bear markets usually precede recessions by nine months.

Bear markets aren't as rare as you might imagine. There have been 26 bear markets in history and they have occurred on the average of less than one every six years.

The typical decline of the major indexes in a bear market is more than −35 percent.

Put those two facts together and once every five to six years you expose yourself and your nest egg to the chance of losing −35 percent. The arithmetic regarding losses of this magnitude isn't pretty, as outlined in Table 1.1.

TABLE 1.1 Bear Market Arithmetic

Amount of Loss	Profit Required to Return to Breakeven
20 percent	25 percent
30 percent	43 percent
50 percent	100 percent

In recent years we have seen "ultra bears"—in 1973–1974 with a decline of −48 percent, 2000–2002 declining −49 percent and 2008 declining −49 percent.

Recovery from these bear markets can be long and hard. On average, since 1929, the time to reach breakeven has been more than five years, however this time can be much, much longer. The 1929 bear market took 25 years to breakeven, the 1973–1974 bear market took more than 8 years to break even.

From 2000 to 2010, the market has still not managed to hold onto its previous highs, and investors have endured a negative rate of return for more than ten years as we went from the Tech Wreck to momentary new highs and then into The Great Recession of 2008.

In 2010, we heard a lot about the "lost decade" since the S&P 500 generated a negative rate of return between 2000 and 2010. However, it wasn't the first secular bear market nor will it likely be the last. The most famous bear was the 1929 crash that lasted more than 20 years. Less famous is the bear that ran from 1966 to 1982, a period of 17 years, and as I write this in early 2010, we are still not back to break even from the bear that began in 2000.

Over the course of the last 80 years we have had three secular bear markets lasting a total of 48 years. Put another way, someone who began investing in 1929 has spent 60 percent of his investing career in bear markets with negative or only slightly positive returns to show for his or her efforts.

Figure 1.1 shows what a typical bear market looks like.

In the chart in Figure 1.1 it's easy to see the devastating drop of the S&P 500 between the beginning of 2008 and the March, 2009 lows. And this type of action isn't so unusual if we look a little farther back at the Tech Wreck of 2000–2002 as shown in Figure 1.2.

Comparing the two charts, a couple of interesting facts immediately stand out. Both bear markets started from approximately 1500 on the S&P, only nearly a decade apart from each other.

FIGURE 1.1 Bear Market of 2008
Chart courtesy of www.StockCharts.com

The 2000 Tech Wreck declined approximately −48 percent over 3.5 months while the Bear Market of 2008 declined a total of approximately −55 percent over five months.

And the subsequent rebounds look very similar when put side by side. Figure 1.3 shows what the last ten years look like altogether:

In Figure 1.3 we can see how in very real terms the stock market, as measured by the S&P 500, has generated a negative rate of return since 2000. And for many investors who tend to buy high and sell low, the returns have been much, much lower.

Of course, the picture becomes even bleaker when you factor inflation into the picture and the lost opportunity costs of nearly a decade of your investing life.

FIGURE 1.2   Tech Wreck
Chart courtesy of StockCharts.com

FIGURE 1.3   Ten Year Chart of S&P 500
Chart courtesy of StockCharts.com

CONCLUSION

So after looking at the last ten years, the obvious questions must be, "Isn't there a better way to invest than what is put forth by 'conventional wisdom?'" And "what would your investment returns look like if you could consistently dodge bear market bites?"

The point here is plain and simple. For investors pursuing a buy and hold strategy, it's a matter of when, and not if, another bear market comes along and takes a big bite out of their portfolio.

In today's high-velocity markets, where money travels around the world at literally the speed of light, it becomes vital to have a plan to survive and prosper in a world that has changed and possibly changed forever.

Unless you believe in a stock market that can only go up and so will somehow magically take you to your investing goals, the obvious conclusion is that all in all, it would be a good idea to avoid bear markets and protect your capital so you'll have more to grow during upswings in the market.

The purpose of this book is to outline practical methods designed to give you a chance to make that seemingly elusive goal a reality.

CHAPTER 2

The Fairy Tale of Buy and Hold

B uy and hold is possibly the most dangerous and damaging piece of advice ever given to investors around the world.

How many times have you heard words like this?

"Buy and hold is the best way to go."

"Hang on, it'll come back."

"What would happen if you missed the ten best days in the market?"

In the next few pages we'll dig into the dangers and pitfalls of "buy and hold."

TEN YEARS OF NEGATIVE RETURNS

Does ten years of negative returns sound like a really great idea? On October 19, 2009, the Dow Jones Industrial Average crossed 10,000 on its way up from the historic March lows of 6,547, and the 10,000 milestone was met with the predictable gushing and cheerleading in the financial press. But what was less heralded was the fact that the Dow had previously crossed the 10,000 barrier for the first time on March 29, 1999, more than ten years earlier.

So, in essence, buy and hold investors in the major index averages, a view often touted as a low-cost, efficient way to invest in the stock market, had just subjected themselves to ten years of no returns.

So let's think about this for a moment. If you were a salesperson and didn't grow your territory for ten years, do you think you'd still have a job? If you went from March 1999 to October 2009 without getting a raise or a promotion, it's highly likely that you would be less than happy with your employer or well on your way to greener pastures.

And so it remains something of a mystery as to why we continue to hear the familiar bromides of the financial experts touting the benefits of buy and hold.

Why does this continue?

I don't know, but the fact of the matter is that this one piece of poor advice has cost investors trillions of dollars in profits.

Between 1999 and 2010, buy and hold investors lost money. This sad statistic is further compounded by the fact that study after study show that most retail investors actually underperform even the major indexes because of their propensity to buy high and sell low.

Buyers of individual stocks have fared little better and I'm sure that if you talked to holders of MCI, Enron, U.S. Airways, General Motors, CIT, Bear Stearns, Fannie Mae, Freddie Mac and AIG, among others, they would tell you that buy and hold didn't work out too well for them, either.

Supply and demand is a basic economic fact and rule that applies to all markets. When supply exceeds demand, prices go down. When demand exceeds supply, prices go up. This works in real estate, employment, or any commodity market. The trick is to know whether supply or demand is the dominant force in the marketplace and then what to do about it.

If there is more supply than demand, prices will go down, and you want to be selling before that happens or at least before too much selling has taken hold and saddled you with a big loss. If there's more demand than supply, prices will go up, and you want to be in the market soon after they start climbing.

Buying and holding is like wearing your swimsuit year-round and standing by your pool. You'll be fine in summer, but when winter comes, you'll get frostbite.

You wouldn't think of driving a car with no hands or wearing a swimsuit on a ski vacation, so why would you consider one fixed strategy for rapidly changing financial markets and economic conditions?

A buy and hold investor has no regard for fundamental economic rules like supply and demand and so he puts himself at risk before irrevocable forces in the marketplace. If demand is in control of the markets, he's in good shape because prices will go up, but if supply has the upper hand, he is destined to lose and perhaps lose significantly and for long periods of time.

So in my opinion, buy and hold is a highly risky strategy.

The idea that you can buy a stock or mutual fund and hold it for ten or twenty or thirty years and automatically come out a winner is simple and appealing. Just buy and hold. Nothing to it. Because over time the market always goes up, and so the only possible outcome is a positive return.

Buy and hold could be an acceptable strategy if you have twenty or thirty or more years to wait for the market to "come back" after a decline. But how many people have 30 years? Plus, there's no guarantee that 30 years is any kind of magic number.

Over shorter periods, bonds have outperformed stocks and the sobering fact that we all face is that most people don't have thirty years. Even for someone just starting out, it's highly unlikely that most investors could hang on for thirty years through the ups and downs of volatile markets.

Buy and hold is the lazy man's way to try to invest in the stock market. The truth is that there is no easy way to make money in the stock market, particularly since the onset of The Great Recession.

Buy and hold is lazy and it is easy. A financial advisor doesn't have to learn anything about money management or risk management or trading or technical or even fundamental analysis to put you in a buy and hold investment. Just buy a mutual fund or ETF and hang on and the market will save you and everything will be fine and the advisor can earn his fee for doing nothing. A good set-up if there ever was one.

In a long term bull market, this approach works fine. But with two major bear markets in the last ten years, buy and hold is a risky strategy at best and downright dangerous at worst.

As you can see in Figure 2.1, over the past ten years, buy and hold has gone nowhere and very likely has gone backwards for a couple of reasons.

First of all, retail investors tend to get out at market bottoms and then they tend not to come back until far into the rally, if at all, and so actually underperform in buy and hold.

The second reason is inflation because with nominal inflation rates of 2 to 3 percent a year, these indexes have actually generated significant negative rates of return over the past ten years.

In both the Tech Wreck and The Great Recession, people watched helplessly as their nest eggs imploded by huge double-digit percentages.

Finally, if and when the indexes ever get back to their previous nominal highs, many investors will still be 20 percent or more in the hole because of the effects of inflation on their stagnant portfolios over the course of ten or more years.

IMPACT ON RETIREMENT

Retirement plans have been devastated, families have been mauled, college choices limited because of the two vicious bear markets that hit during the decade between 2000 and 2010, and this pain will likely continue for years

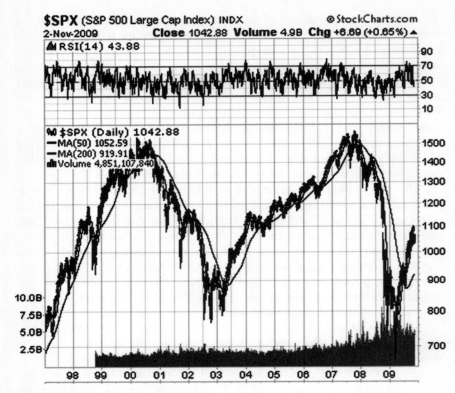

FIGURE 2.1   S&P 500 1999–2009
Chart courtesy of StockCharts.com

to come as people struggle to recover from the destruction their net worth encountered during the Bear Market of 2008, the worst bear market since the Great Depression.

And just because it looks like the Fed managed to avoid a "depression," it doesn't mean that a bear market can't happen again. Just check out a couple of recent declines and what they have meant for investors. Figure 2.2 graphically depicts the horror of Black Monday, October 19, 1987, when the Dow Jones Industrials suffered its worst percentage drop in history.

In Figure 2.3 (see p. 14) we see the whipsaws that rippled through the Dow Jones Industrials during 2000 at the start of the Tech Wreck. And in Figure 2.4 (see p. 15) we see the Tech Wreck and its devastation.

Of course, stock market crashes and reversals aren't limited to the United States. Figure 2.5 (see p. 16) clearly depicts what has happened in Japan over twenty-plus years.

FIGURE 2.2 Dow Jones Industrials 1987
Chart courtesy of StockCharts.com

The Nikkei clearly points out a possibility that we are mostly unfamiliar with: Bear markets can last for decades. In 1990, the Nikkei Index was north of 30,000 and in late 2009, it stands below a paltry 10,000, approximately one-third of its former value.

Declines like these are particularly devastating for people in retirement or near retirement and that's why The Great Recession will have such a long-lasting effect on American society. The Great Recession came along in 2008 at precisely the time when the massive juggernaut of the baby boom generation should have been in their peak earnings and investment years.

But instead of accumulating wealth in their 401ks and home equity, what happened was that their home values were destroyed in the housing crunch, their portfolios were smashed in the bear market, and many people were thrown out of work, downsized, or found themselves

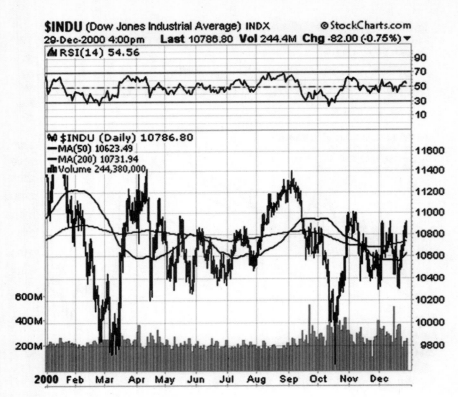

FIGURE 2.3 Dow Jones 2000
Chart courtesy of StockCharts.com

working for reduced wages at just the time they should have really been making hay.

The result is predictable: More and more people have had to put off retirement and work longer than they had planned. Many will not have as much money for retirement as they expected, and many will not be able to retire at all.

Overall, baby boomers approaching retirement age have experienced a drastic decline in their standard of living during what should have been their peak earnings years and they can expect to be able to have less money for vacations and dinners out and entertainment when they hit their "golden years."

The impact of the bear market is real and long lasting, and even more so in today's world where so many traditional defined benefit plans have been replaced by 401ks.

FIGURE 2.4 Tech Wreck 2000–2003
Chart courtesy of StockCharts.com

More problems related to buy and hold exist in the 401k world. Nearly half of workers over age 55 have less than $50,000 in savings and most eligible workers don't contribute annually to a 401k because they don't have enough income to make ends meet and still contribute to their retirement accounts.

So let's take a hypothetical example of a guy approaching retirement who saw his 401k decline from $800,000 to $500,000 during The Great Recession and associated bear market. Using a standard rule of thumb of extracting 5 percent of a retirement account's value to fund retirement, he would have had $40,000 in annual income before the bear market but now only has $25,000 to withdraw each year from his depleted principal balance. So this leads to a lot of bad choices such as having to work longer, sell one's house, send the wife back to work, or move in with the kids.

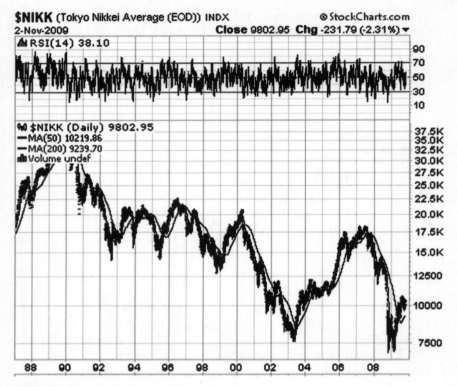

FIGURE 2.5 The Nikkei Index 1988–Present
Chart courtesy of StockCharts.com

You can clearly see why buy and hold is a dangerous gambit and why it's imperative to find a better way.

Popular financial press and theories will tell you that it's "impossible to beat the market," but I know for sure that simply isn't true. I personally know managers who consistently "beat the market" and you'll meet some of these people later in the book and gain some insights into how they're able to do what most pundits say is impossible.

I know for sure that they're not smarter than you or me, but they are more knowledgeable, far more knowledgeable than the average retail investor. They have educated themselves and learned their craft. They have a trading plan. They run their trading like a business and they have the discipline to stick with their plan through thick and thin.

There's no reason in the world that you can't do the same thing. And if you do, whether using the techniques outlined in this book or finding other techniques well suited to your personality, you'll find yourself very likely sleeping better and building your net worth faster and more efficiently than ever before.

You'll also be able to avoid this long litany of sad facts:

- At of the end of 2009, the major market indexes are still well below their ten-year highs, meaning investors have lost ten years of their investment lives.
- In addition to not realizing any capital gains, investors have lost purchasing power of more than 20 percent due to the constant march of inflation.
- A decline of 50 percent like we experienced in 2009 requires a gain of 100 percent just to break even.

In my view, buy and hold is a lot like driving your car without insurance. You are out on a limb, exposed to unlimited liability, and are very simply an accident waiting to happen over and over again.

As a buy and hold investor, you're saying that you're willing to let your future be controlled by market forces rather than taking charge of your own destiny. You're willing to let the law of averages determine what kind of retirement you're going to have, and if you're unlucky enough to match up your best earning and savings years with a bear market decline, the outcome will not be positive.

Worse yet, if you're already retired, a huge decline could easily result in your running out of money before you die. And that would be the worst of all worlds.

However, there is an alternative, and that of course is active management, whether you call it "market timing" or "trading," dirty words in Wall Street's lexicon. I call it active management or tactical management and in my view it's a terrific way to sidestep bear market declines and so preserve your capital and allow you to outperform the market during good times.

Warren Buffett got it right when he said there are only two rules of investing:

Rule No. 1: Don't lose money
Rule No. 2: Don't forget rule #1.[1]

That's what active portfolio management is all about, because if you don't lose money during downturns like we saw in 2008, then you can move ahead when the bull market returns, as it inevitably will. Plus, if you don't lose money during downturns, you only have to capture roughly 30 percent of the upside move of a bull market to beat buy and hold. This fact alone allows you to maximize your gains while minimizing your exposure to market risk and drawdowns.

You can "invest for the long run," as so many financial pundits would have you do, or you can deploy a tactical trading plan designed to take advantage of rapidly changing financial and market conditions. I prefer the tactical option because "investing for the long run" reminds me of famed economist John Maynard Keynes who said, "In the long run, we're all dead."[2]

THE WORLD IS CHANGING

Most professional money managers and brokers have long been supporters of "buy and hold" because it's inexpensive and it's easy. However, after the carnage of the most recent bear market, many advisers are beginning to look for a better way to manage their clients' assets.

An article from the Wall Street Journal Digital Network reported that "about 15 percent of the 500 advisors polled by consulting firm GDS Research LLC of Sherborn, Massachusetts, and Practical Perspectives LLC of Boxford, Massachusetts, say they've made significant changes in the ways they manage money."[3]

Will Hepburn, Chairman of the National Association of Active Investment Managers (NAAIM) and President of Hepburn Capital Management told me that "buy and hold is not for everybody because it's a very high risk strategy. Just look at the drawdowns a buy and hold account experiences."

I asked Will if he had seen a change in investment advisors' attitudes towards active trading and tactical management, and he replied, "Since the bear market began, we've had a surge in membership and inquiries from advisors. The Great American Investment Creed is to buy low and sell high, but few advisors had any idea about when their clients should sell. Now many of them are looking to the NAAIM Survey of Manager Sentiment for guidance. I call it the 'NAAIM Number' and it's the average exposure to the stock market across our membership that's reported in a weekly survey. A growing number of advisors now realize that more bear markets are a real possibility and they need a way to know when it's time to be in the market and when it's time to be out."

CONCLUSION

In summary, the crowd that always preached buying a mix of stocks, bonds, and cash and then holding those investments forever is changing its tune as a result of the Great Recession. The reason for this evolving attitude is clearly evident if you just take a quick glance at Figure 2.6. Over the last ten years, the major U.S. indexes have experienced a "Lost Decade" of negative returns.

Many would argue that this "Lost Decade" is an ongoing secular bear market that has many years to run, and if that is the case, "buy and hold" very likely won't get you where you want to go and perhaps active management or tactical management could offer a better alternative.

Of course, there are many pitfalls in active trading that we'll discuss as we work our way through this problem; pitfalls like higher trading costs, increased taxes, the very real chance of "blowing up" and ongoing problems of transparency and liquidity in alternative products like hedge funds and private capital investments.

But in my mind, buy and hold has been a losing strategy for a very long time and that's a good enough reason to try to find a different and possibly better approach. Add in the Great Recession and the mission becomes even more urgent.

Just because apparently we've stepped back from the brink this time around, the historical fact cannot be avoided that once every six years you will very likely be faced with an economic train wreck that can wipe out 40 percent or more of your net worth. But if you can develop and successfully execute a trading and investing plan that fits your lifestyle and temperament, you can do better, in my opinion.

Not that this is an easy task to accomplish by any means, especially for people who have busy lives and jobs and families and don't want to make a job out of managing their money. But there are many alternatives for the do-it-yourselfer who just wants to sidestep bear markets, as well as for people who want to actively manage and trade their accounts.

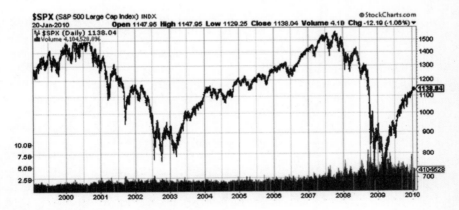

FIGURE 2.6 The Lost Decade
Chart courtesy of StockCharts.com

The options range from being a day trader, working every minute in front of your computer screen, to having your money run by professional money managers and putting your portfolio on autopilot. Whatever choice is right for you is the important thing to determine.

But even more important is that you actually go through the process and do something so that you can avoid "The Lost Decade" that so many investors have experienced.

CHAPTER 3

Four More Wall Street Fairy Tales: Conventional Wisdom That Could Cost You Money

I n this chapter we're going to look at some of Wall Street's favorite bromides for investment success and see why they might not be effective or even safe.

We're going to be taking a look at slogans and statements we've all heard a thousand times as being the gateway to investment nirvana and success:

- "Asset Allocation"
- "Dollar Cost Averaging"
- "The Market Goes Up 8 percent a Year"
- "Sell the Leaders, Buy the Laggards"

These are Wall Street Sacred Cows and we're going to take a look at why they might be flawed, even dangerous, in today's fast-moving markets.

IS ASSET ALLOCATION THE ANSWER?

Asset allocation is a standard approach to investing that says you should diversify between stocks, bonds, gold, and so on, and its goal is to offer protection in down markets while yielding upside potential.

Typically based on age, most asset allocation strategies get more conservative the older you get.

The most common asset allocation theory is the 60/40 Theory in which you put 60 percent of your assets in stock and 40 percent in bonds. And yet another is the 120 Theory which says you should subtract your age from 120 and that percentage should be the amount you invest in stocks. So for a 50-year old, 70 percent should be in stocks and 30 percent in bonds and for a 70-year old, you'd be at 50/50 percent.

On the surface, there's nothing wrong with this principal as long as you realize the risks that are inherent in these methods of traditional asset allocation.

The first risk is the threat of inflation. With bonds currently delivering miniscule rates of return, it's very likely that you won't even keep up with inflation and will steadily lose purchasing power as time goes on.

The second risk to bonds is interest rate risk. As you know, bond prices move opposite to interest rates and with interest rates near zero as we come out of The Great Recession of 2008, it seems likely that they have nowhere to go but up and so your principal could be at risk as rates rise.

Further risks to bond investors come to those who buy into bond funds. Unlike a bond which offers a specific interest rate for a specific period of time, after which your principal is returned, a bond fund offers neither of these features. The interest rate can change and so can the Net Asset Value dependent on the action of interest rates. If rates go up, your NAV will go down, thus you will lose principal.

And finally, traditional views of asset allocation may not provide you with any diversification at all.

The Bear Market of 2008 was a case in point as almost every asset class became correlated and moved in tandem. So instead of having the protection they thought they had, investors, advisors and financial planners saw all of their equity asset classes losing value at the same time.

In 2008, the S&P 500 lost more than −30 percent, major international markets in Europe and Asia tumbled more than −40 percent, real estate investment trusts plunged more than −30 percent while high-yield bonds lost in the mid −20 percent range and commodities dropped more than −35 percent.

So there really was nowhere to hide except in cash, in short positions, or by actively trading your portfolio to take advantage of the declining assets around the world. All in all, traditional asset allocation may not be the cure all it's presented to be and it's easy to see how millions of investors have pinned their hopes on flawed models.

We'll wrap up our discussion of asset allocation by listening to legendary investor and second richest man in the world, Warren Buffett, who once said, "Wide diversification is only required when investors do not understand what they are doing."[1]

THE FAIRY TALES REVEALED

Let's take a closer look at the fairy tales of "dollar cost averaging," "the market goes up 8 percent a year," and "sell the leaders, buy the laggards." These look good on paper but do they work?

Dollar Cost Averaging

Like so many Wall Street bromides for investment success, dollar cost averaging sounds good to the average investor. Basically the theory is that you invest a fixed amount of money over a long period of time and so are buying stocks or mutual funds at varying prices, both high and low, as the market fluctuates.

And this sounds good. Since it can be automatic, you don't have to time the market, and you average your cost basis in hopes of making profits over time. It makes sense if you buy more shares over time at lower prices and fewer shares at higher prices, as you decrease your overall cost basis.

Most brokers and investment salespeople like the idea because it sets them up on a steady growth path for their assets under management and it's easier to talk someone out of a few dollars per month than a lump sum up front. However, numerous academic studies have proven that dollar cost averaging is in fact a flawed concept and that lump sum investing is actually a superior way to invest.

In fact, according to Dr. Michael S. Rozeff in his article, "Lump Sum Investing versus Dollar Cost Averaging," those who hesitate, lose, over a sixty-five year period, lump-sum investing will outperform dollar cost averaging two thirds of the time and generate a higher return of 1 to 4 percent per year as the stock size declines. Dr. Rozeff goes on to say that "to spread one's investment over time simply invites higher standard deviation of return without an increase in expected return."[2]

The bottom line is that lump-sum investing has been statistically proven to offer the best returns while dollar cost averaging was less effective. Interestingly, taking a random investment approach and putting in money on no set schedule, produced investment returns in a range between those of lump sum and dollar cost averaging.

The Market Goes Up 8 Percent A Year

How many times have you read that the markets go up 8 percent a year on average? I've read this a lot and I'm always amazed because it sounds so good to think that all you have to do to make money in the markets is to buy stocks and over time you'll be rewarded with almost automatic gains.

This might be true if you look back to the beginning of time, but most of us aren't elephants that have eighty or more years to invest in the markets and recover whatever losses we might encounter. Furthermore, as we discussed earlier, there are many periods of years and even decades where the markets don't go up 8 percent per year and even decline. If you need your money during one of these periods, you could be in real trouble.

Sell the Leaders, Buy the Laggards

This is another favorite Wall Street sermon that endangers your nest egg. Buying a stock when it's cheap doesn't necessarily spell out a successful investment.

For instance, a high-flying tech stock like JDS Uniphase was selling for $875 per share in 1999 and then fell to $80/share in 2002 towards the end of the Tech Wreck, a decline of approximately 90 percent. An investor thinking that this was a screaming deal would be looking at his JDS Uniphase "laggard" priced today in the mid $5 range, a further decline of more than 90 percent.

Just because a stock is a leader doesn't mean it will stop being a leader and just because a stock is a laggard doesn't necessarily make it a budding leader down the road. In fact, in his book *The Seven Rules of Wall Street; Crash Tested Investment Strategies That Beat the Market*, Sam Stovall, Chief Investment Strategist at Standard and Poor's Equity Research, points out that buying last year's winners at the beginning of every year between 1970 and 2007 outperformed the S&P 500 in compound growth by nearly 80 percent (13.7 percent versus 7.6 percent) and the winners beat the losers in seven out of every ten years.[3]

Clearly, "sell the leaders, buy the laggards" is more fairy tale than fact, but sadly, many investors are betting their futures on this bit of flawed conventional wisdom.

CONCLUSION

In these last few pages, we've taken a look at Wall Street "conventional wisdom" as it relates to concepts like "Buy and Hold," "Asset Allocation," "The Market Goes Up 8 percent A Year," "Dollar Cost Averaging" and "Sell the Leaders, Buy the Laggards."

The essential premise of the book you're reading now is that Wall Street doesn't care one wit about you or your future. Virtually no one on

Wall Street or in the financial media has a clue about what they're doing and most of the "rules" and "conventional wisdom" are at the least, useless, and at the worst, fatally flawed.

This chapter wraps up Part 1 of our journey, "Five Wall Street Fairy Tales and Why the Conventional Wisdom is Flawed." Through these pages we've looked at the problems most investors face and now it's time to turn our attention to possible solutions and a better way forward through today's difficult times.

PART II

Why Exchange Traded Funds?

I n today's complex financial markets, investors have literally dozens of different investment vehicles from which to choose. We can buy stocks, bonds, mutual funds. We can buy options and futures contracts, we can trade forex and we can short stocks and get even more complicated by combining strategies between options and equities or Exchange Traded Funds.

As I looked across the universe of potential investments, I settled on Exchange Traded Funds for a number of compelling reasons and in this section we're going to review the facts and features that make Exchange Traded Funds such an attractive option for investors and traders alike.

I'm not alone in this determination, as ETFs have exploded over the past decade, both in numbers and volume. Still, many individual investors have not even heard of them today, which is amazing to me, and they have yet to catch up with mutual fund volume or assets under management, although I think that day is not too far away.

For investors, traders and people interested in trading, Exchange Traded Funds allow you a myriad of opportunities ranging from long-term buy and hold strategies in plain vanilla index funds, to high velocity day trading in Exchange Traded Funds that offer triple leverage to the underlying index.

So let's jump into the world of Exchange Traded Funds, also known as ETFs, and see exactly what these exciting products have to offer.

CHAPTER 4

History and Growth of Exchange Traded Funds

T he first Exchange Traded Fund, or ETF, was born in 1990, and little did anyone know that this new product would take off on a meteoric growth curve that would change the face of investing forever.

FROM ZERO TO 836 IN 19 SHORT YEARS

The first ETF emerged on the Toronto Stock Exchange in 1990 and migrated to America in 1993. The first ETF in America was launched in January 1993: the Standard and Poor's Deposit Receipt, symbol (SPY) and affectionately known in investing circles as the "Spider." It was designed to track the Standard and Poor's 500 Index and today is still the largest ETF in existence with more than $66 billion in assets as of February 2010.

ETFs started life predominantly as an institutional product but quickly spread to individual investors as their positive features and benefits became apparent and more widely known.

What's an ETF?

An ETF is the clever combination of the characteristics of a mutual fund with a single stock investment. It's a financial instrument that looks like a mutual fund but trades like a stock.

29

ETFs are similar to mutual funds because most are made up of a basket of stocks that track a particular sector like Real Estate or Health Care and they also track major indexes like the Dow, NASDAQ, and S&P 500.

ETFs offer a seemingly limitless palette of choices and their variety expands nearly on a daily basis. Today you can find ETFs that follow international indexes, country specific indexes and commodities, and even specific subsectors like currencies, steel, coal or solar energy.

Growth of Exchange Traded Funds

Since those early days in 1993, when the ETF universe started with one domestic fund, ETFs have exploded on the investing scene. Every day it seems new ETFs are coming to market and even The Great Recession could only slow down, but not stop, their overall growth. By the end of 2009, there were more than 830 individual offerings in the United States and more than 1,600 worldwide.

According to Morningstar, total U.S. ETF assets stood at $746.9 billion at the end of January 2010, and experienced a 49.2 percent growth rate on a year-over-year basis.[1] Worldwide, ETF assets climbed past the $1 trillion mark in 2009, up 45 percent for the year, according to a recent article in the Wall Street Journal Digital Network.[2]

ETFs Bring Significant Value to the Table

The dramatic growth of ETFs can be easily explained by the fact that they offer investors significant advantages over either mutual fund or single stock investing. In fact, they offer the "best of both worlds" and open doors to investment arenas like currencies and commodities that have previously been unavailable to retail investors.

Let's take a look at some of the features unique to Exchange Traded Funds that account for their fast growth and wide popularity:

ETFs Offer Immediate Diversification   Like a mutual fund, ETFs invest in a block of securities and the investor receives shares in the fund he or she selects. This offers you instant diversification since you own a basket of stocks rather than just one that could go bankrupt and cause you to lose your entire investment.

Plus, with the wide selection of asset classes available through ETFs, the investor gains immediate access to a wide range of investment possibilities and can design his own portfolio however he or she sees fit. This capability offers you the opportunity for wide diversification in a simple, easy-to-manage format. ETFs are a convenient, cost-effective way to build a portfolio according to whatever asset allocation guidelines you want to follow.

ETFs Are Less Expensive Than Mutual Funds As we just discussed, ETFs offer all of the benefits provided by mutual funds but they do so at a much lower cost. Typical mutual fund expenses can run as high as 1.5 percent in a managed fund while ETFs sport expense ratios of as low as 0.10 percent for (SPY) the SPDR S&P 500 ETF. Also with an ETF you don't pay load fees nor do you have the management fees that come with actively managed mutual funds.

ETFs Offer Tax Advantages Over Mutual Funds ETFs can be more tax efficient than mutual funds for several reasons. They typically have low turnover—and so fewer taxable gains—and you can choose ETFs that don't have large capital gains distributions or dividends.

Furthermore, the big advantage ETFs have over mutual funds is that you're only liable for taxes on the shares you own. If a mutual fund manager liquidates positions, the remaining shareholders get hit for the gains incurred. It's possible to get taxed on gains you never made if you entered the fund late in the year and then the fund issues gains. On the contrary, when you own an ETF, you don't have to pay taxes or dividends unless you own the ETF on the date payment is declared.

ETFs Act Like Stocks ETFs act like stocks in that you can trade them exactly in the same way you can trade stocks and with the same features. You can buy an ETF on margin. You can option an ETF, write covered calls, and employ all of the same kinds of order entries and exits like limit orders or stop losses. You can short an ETF and can buy or sell them anytime during the trading day. Basically, you can do anything with most ETFs that you can with an individual stock. In Table 4.1, we can see a graphical comparison of an Exchange Traded Fund to a single stock or mutual fund investment.

TABLE 4.1 Features of ETS Compared to Single Stock and Mutual Fund Investments

Feature	Exchange Traded Fund	Individual Stock	Mutual Fund
Available for purchase in IRA or 401K Plans	Yes	Yes	Yes
Marginable	Yes	Yes	No
Options can be purchased on the underlying asset	Yes	Yes	No
Can buy or sell continuously while markets are open	Yes	Yes	No
Carry redemption charges or short-term withdrawal fees	No	No	Quite often

It's quite obvious that ETFs offer enormous flexibility and advantages over either individual stocks or mutual funds. They also offer complete pricing transparency. At any given time you know exactly what the price and value of your investment is as opposed to mutual funds that typically only publish prices once a day after the market closes.

CONCLUSION

In this chapter we've seen some of the advantages that Exchange Traded Funds offer compared to traditional mutual funds. In the next chapter we'll take a look at the different types of ETFs that are available to us as traders and investors.

CHAPTER 5

Types of Exchange Traded Funds

I n this chapter we're going to take a look at the major classes of Exchange Traded Funds and their advantages, disadvantages, and potential pitfalls. We'll start with plain vanilla standard Exchange Traded Funds and work our way into the most exotic offerings on the market today.

The list of ETFs is almost endless and in fact presents an unexpected challenge to novice and experienced investors and traders alike: ETF Overload. I know that might sound a little silly but it is a real problem and can hurt performance dramatically if you try to track and trade too many of these funds at one time.

When I first started Wall Street Sector Selector, I tracked and traded over 150 ETFs and it was so exciting to have all of these possibilities for profit stretching before me. But over the months and years, I found myself getting burned out and confused and simply unable to keep up with the new funds that seemed to be popping up every day.

Diversification is an important tenet of investment and trading success, but over the years, I've learned that the best strategy is to take a sample of the various ETFs and limit your focus to just a few. You'll see what I mean as we go along through this section.

I've come to the conclusion that it's better to be a specialist than a generalist and that it's better to be a one-trick pony, as long as it's a good trick.

STANDARD EXCHANGE TRADED FUNDS

ETFs have been around for more than fifteen years, but amazingly, many investors still don't know about them or the almost limitless range of choices they offer. But as the fastest-growing area of the investing universe, it's a subject you need to understand and so we'll go into some detail about what they are, how they work, and how we can use them to reach our financial goals.

When you buy an ETF, you're buying a pool of securities that are bundled into one entity for pricing and trading purposes.

You can buy indexes like the S&P or the Dow Jones Industrials; you can buy sectors like gold, oil, or agriculture; you can buy style like Large Cap or Small Cap Value; you can buy foreign currencies like the Eurodollar or Swiss Franc; you can even buy exotic commodities like Water or Wind Power. You can even buy ETFs that move inversely, or opposite, to an index like the Dow or S&P and so effectively short the market if you think it's going down. This offers investors tremendous flexibility and inverse ETFs can even be used within IRA and 401k accounts which don't allow traditional short selling.

In general, it's best to focus on a few different types of ETFs and find the ones that are the best weapons in your arsenal. For almost every investor or trader, Index Funds are oftentimes the bedrock of their trading toolkit. Let's take a look at the most widely used and useful.

INDEX FUNDS

Index funds are far and away the most popular of the Exchange Traded Funds and there are virtually an unlimited number available from which to choose. However, in my opinion, most investors and traders would be well served to focus on just the following major ETFs for index exposure.

- *SPDR S&P 500 Index (SPY):* the "Big Kahuna" of all ETFs that allows you to track the S&P 500 which is the index of the 500 largest domestic U.S. stocks and is often considered to be a proxy for the U.S. Stock Market.
- *Diamonds Trust Series 1 (DIA):* Also known as the "Diamonds," this tracks the Dow Jones Industrial Average which is the index of large blue chip stocks and tracks 30 of America's biggest and most prominent companies.
- *PowerShares QQQ (QQQQ):* Known as "the Qs," this ETF tracks the NASDAQ 100 which is the largest 100 stocks that are not financially related in the NASDAQ index.

- *iShares MSCI Emerging Markets Index (EEM):* which gives you access to emerging country stock markets like Brazil, Korea, Russia, China, and India, some of the fastest growing sectors in the world.
- *iShares Russell 2000 (IWM):* Also known as "the Russell," this index allows you to invest in 2,000 small cap companies.

MARKET CAP AND STYLE FUNDS

If you're looking for a nearly unlimited number of market cap and investment style funds, you've found the right place with ETFs. From the major providers you can choose from Small Caps, Mid Caps, Dow 30, Russell 2000, Russell 3000, Russell 1000, Russell 1000 Value, Russell 1000 Growth, Russell MidCap Value, Russell Microcap Index, and S&P Midcap Growth, among others.

BOND FUNDS

In recent years, there has been a proliferation of Bond ETFs coming to market, perhaps in response to the fact that so many investors have been burned so badly in the stock market and are looking for the relative safety and stability of a fixed income investment vehicle.

Like the Market Cap and Style Funds, a blizzard of ETFs awaits the investor/trader interested in participating in this arena. One can choose from short term, long term, inverse funds that move opposite to the price of the underlying bond, Treasuries of all stripes, even TIPS (Treasury Inflation Protected Securities) and Municipal Bonds.

SECTOR EXCHANGE TRADED FUNDS

Exposure to various sectors is one of the most compelling reasons to consider ETFs for your investing or trading activities. Through these flexible and innovative products, you can gain exposure to almost any sector you can think of.

Here's just a partial list from a couple of the major providers:

iShares Family

(ICF) Cohen and Steer Realty Index Fund
(ITA) Dow Jones U.S. Aerospace and Defense Index Fund
(IYT) Dow Jones Transportation Average

(IYM) Dow Jones U.S. Basic Materials Sector Index Fund
(IYK) Dow Jones U.S. Consumer Goods Index Fund
(IYE) Dow Jones U.S. Energy Sector Index
(IYF) Dow Jones U.S. Financial Sector Index
(IHF) Dow Jones U.S. HealthCare Providers Index
(ITB) Dow Jones U.S. Home Construction Index
(IAK) Dow Jones U.S. Insurance Index
(IEO) Dow Jones U.S. Oil and Gas Exploration
(IYR) Dow Jones U.S. Real Estate Index
(IAT) Dow Jones U.S. Regional Banks Index
(IDU) Dow Jones U.S. Utilities Index

State Street Global: SPDR Sector ETFs

XLF: SPDR Select Sector Fund—Financial
XLB: SPDR Select Sector Fund—Basic
KBE: SPDR KBW Bank ETF
XLY: SPDR Select Sector Fund
RWX: SPDR DJ Wilshire Intl Real Estate
RWR: SPDR DJ Wilshire REIT ETF
XRT: SPDR S&P Retail ETF
GLD: SPDR Gold Trust
XLE: SPDR Select Sector Fund—Energy sector
XLK: SPDR Select Sector Fund—Tech
XLU: SPDR Select Sector Fund—Utilities
XLV: SPDR Select Sector Fund—Health
XLP: SPDR Select Sector Fund—Construction
XLI: SPDR Select Sector Fund—Industrial

GLOBAL REGIONS AND COUNTRY SPECIFIC EXCHANGE TRADED FUNDS

ETFs designed to track the major indexes of various countries and regions have been one of the hottest growth areas in recent years. It's no secret that international markets, particularly the emerging markets, have recently generated returns far superior to the developed world, and so massive wealth has been funneled toward these ETFs.

To me, the vast array of choices in the international arena is one of the most exciting developments in the investment universe in recent years. No longer is a trader/investor limited to the confines of the American Exchanges and this opens a whole range of options previously unavailable to U.S. investors.

Regional and Broad-Based International Exchange Traded Funds

- Vanguard Emerging Markets Stock ETF (VWO)
- iShares MSCI Emerging Markets Index (EEM)
- iShares MSCI Pacific ex-Japan (EPP)
- iShares S&P Latin American 40 Index (ILF)
- iShares MSCI EAFE Index (Europe, Asia, Far East (EFA))
- iShares S&P Europe 350 Index (IEV)

Specific Country Exchange Traded Funds

- iShares FTSE/Xinhua China 25 Index (FXI)
- iShares MSCI Brazil Index (EWZ)
- iShares MSCI South Korea Index (EWY)
- iShares MSCI Taiwan Index (EWT)
- iShares MSCI Japan Index (EWJ)
- iShares Hong Kong Index (EWH)
- iShares Malaysia Index (EWM)
- iShares Singapore Index (EWS)
- iShares Mexico Index (EWW)
- Market Vectors Vietnam Index (VNM)

INVERSE EXCHANGE TRADED FUNDS

Inverse ETFs offer traders and investors the opportunity to "short" the market in a way that they haven't had available until just recently. In the past, to short a market—in other words, place a bet that a stock, index, or ETF was going to decline—you had to short a specific stock or use options strategies or a futures contract.

But with inverse ETFs, you can buy an ETF that is designed to increase in value as the underlying index declines. So for example, if you thought the S&P 500 was going to decline, you could buy the ETF (SH) ProShares Short S&P 500 Index. This ETF is designed to move opposite to the return of the index for a single day.

The other significant difference between an inverse ETF and shorting a stock is that investors/traders can buy an inverse ETF within Individual Retirement Accounts and 401k accounts which typically do not allow shorting of stocks. And a final advantage is that, unlike shorting a stock, you do not need a margin account to buy an inverse ETF.

Inverse ETFs can also be used to hedge a long position within your portfolio without using a stop-loss position because your long position is protected from declines by the inverse ETF. The "gotcha" here is that over time, inverse ETFs can produce substantially different returns than the underlying index due to the fact that they're rebalanced daily and daily returns are compounded.

On the ProShares web site, it states, "ProShares Short S&P 500 seeks daily investment results, before fees and expenses that correspond to the inverse (opposite) of the daily performance of the S&P 500® Index. This ETF seeks a return of -100 percent of the return of an index (target) *for a single day.* Due to the compounding of daily returns, ProShares' returns over periods other than one day will likely differ in amount and possibly direction from the target return for the same period. Investors should monitor their ProShares holdings consistent with their strategies, as frequently as daily. For more on correlation, leverage, and other risks, please read the prospectus."[1]

In my view, inverse ETFs are only suitable for short-term traders because over time, it's very likely they will deviate from the underlying index because of the effects of tracking error and compounding.

Inverse ETFs include the following:

- (RWM) Short Russell 2000: Russell 2000 Index
- (SH) Short S&P 500 Index: S&P 500 Index
- (PSQ) Short QQQQ: NASDAQ 100 Index
- (DOG) Short Dow 30: Dow Jones Industrial Average
- (MYY) Short MidCap 400: S&P MidCap 400 Index
- (SBB) Short SmallCap 600: S&P Small Cap 600 Index
- (EUM) Short MSCI Emerging Markets Index: MSCI Emerging Markets Index
- (EFZ) Short MACI EAFE Index: Europe, Africa, Middle East
- (TBF) Short 20+ Year Treasury: Barclays Capital 20+ Year U.S. Treasury Index
- (SEF) Short Financial ETF: Dow Jones U.S. Financials Index
- (DDG) Short Oil and Gas; Dow Jones U.S. Oil and Gas Index

LEVERAGED EXCHANGE TRADED FUNDS

Leveraged ETFs have all the qualities of standard exchange traded funds but offer the opportunity to leverage your investment by as much as three times your investment.

Leveraged ETFs are offered by several of the large ETF providers and are a rapidly growing asset class. Like standard ETFs, they invest in various stocks and underlying indexes and currencies, almost any type of asset you could think of, but they also invest in futures contracts and Equity Index Swap Agreements to leverage their returns.

Most leveraged exchange traded funds seek to return 200 percent of the performance of the underlying index although even more aggressive vehicles are now available and have gained widespread acceptance in the marketplace. You can also use leveraged ETFs that trade opposite to the underlying index or sector and so allow you to "short" the particular asset class at multiples of 200 or even 300 percent.

The way this works is that let's say we're buying a leveraged S&P 500 Index Fund that is designed to double the performance, up or down of the S&P 500 Index. When the S&P 500 Index moves up, our investments are designed to DOUBLE that move, and when the S&P 500 Index moves down, we should decline in value by double the decline of the S&P.

By using this strategy, investors can reach a couple of different goals and reap benefits not available from regular ETFs or mutual funds. First, you can multiply your returns for the same amount of dollars invested and so accelerate your portfolio's growth. Secondly, you can reduce risk by keeping a larger portion of your assets in cash or diversify more widely because fewer dollars are tied up in each leveraged position.

Of course, when using leverage, risk management and position sizing become even more important than when using standard investments because losses, as well as gains, can be magnified. However, for the knowledgeable investor, leveraged exchange traded funds offer very attractive opportunities for growth and so are used widely by trading professionals and active money managers.

Be Aware of Additional Risks   Leveraged ETFs come with additional risk factors that investor/traders must keep in mind at all times. Aside from the risks of using leverage, which multiplies and amplifies your gains or losses, these funds don't operate in the same manner as standard ETFs.

Unlike standard Exchange Traded Funds, these leveraged ETFs use derivatives, swaps, and futures contracts and so their pricing generally is based on *daily* movements in the price. What this means is that over time, a tracking error tends to develop that can either work for or against you. If the market is moving in your direction, your gains will be compounded and if the market is moving against your position, your losses will be compounded.

The advent of leveraged ETFs has brought with it a flurry of lawsuits and regulatory action to make investors aware of these unusual characteristics and it's imperative that you read the prospectuses carefully as well as the regulatory warnings about these products so that you fully understand what you're getting yourself into. FINRA, the Financial Industry Regulatory Authority, has published numerous comments regarding the use of leveraged ETFs by retail investors and these can be reviewed at the FINRA web site, finra.org.

My view is that these are legitimate and useful products if used correctly in a professionally-managed, carefully monitored program with full understanding of their potential pitfalls. Most experts agree that they're only appropriate for experienced investors/traders who have the risk tolerance to work in this market that's dominated by professionals.

Some examples of 2X leveraged Exchange Traded Funds are:

(QID) UltraShort QQQ: NASDAQ 100
(DXD) UltraShort Dow 30: Dow Jones Industrial Average
(SDS) UltraShort S&P 500: S&P 500 Index
(TWM) UltraShort Russell 2000: Russell 2000 Index
(SKF) UltraShort Financials: Dow Jones U.S. Financials Index
(SRS) UltraShort Real Estate: Dow Jones U.S. Real Estate Index
(REW) UltraShort Technology: Dow Jones U.S. Technology Index
(EEV) UltraShort MSCI Emerging Markets: MSCI Emerging Markets Index
(FXP) UltraShort FTSE/Xinhua China 25: FTSE/Xinhua China 25 Index
(EWV) Ultrashort MSCI Japan: MSCI Japan Index
(SMK) UltraShort MSCI Mexico Investable Market: MSCI Mexico Investable Market Index
(BZQ) UltraShort MSCI Brazil: MSCI Brazil Index
(TBT) Ultrashort 20+ Year Treasury: Barclays Capital 20+ Year U.S. Treasury Index
(CMD) UltraShort DJ-UBS Commodity: Dow Jones-UBS Commodity Index
(SCO) UltraShort DJ-UBS Crude Oil: Dow Jones-UBS Crude Oil Sub-Index
(GLL) UltraShort Gold: Gold
(ZSL) UltraShort Silver: Silver

Some examples of 3X leveraged Exchange Traded Funds are:

(BGU) Daily Large Cap Bull 3X Shares: Russell 1000
(TNA) Daily Small Cap Bull 3X Shares: Russell 2000
(ERX) Daily Energy Bull 3X Shares: Russell 1000 Energy
(FAS) Daily Financial Bull 3X Shares: Russell 1000 Financial Services
(DRN) Daily Real Estate Bull 3X Shares: MSCI U.S. REIT Index
(TYH) Daily Technology Bull 3X Shares: Russell 1000 Technology Index
(DZK) Daily Developed Markets Bull 3X Shares: MSCI EAFE Index

(EDC) Daily Emerging Markets Bull 3X Shares: MSCI Emerging Markets Index

(TYD) Daily 10-Year Treasury Bull 3X Shares: NYSE ARCA Current 10-Year U.S. Treasury Index

(TMF) Daily 20-Year Treasury Bull 3X Shares: NYSE ARCA Current 30-Year U.S. Treasury Index

(BGZ) Daily Large Cap Bear 3X Shares: Russell 1000

(MWN) Daily Mid Cap Bear 3X Shares: Russell Midcap Index

(TZA) Daily Small Cap Bear 3X Shares: Russell 2000

(ERY) Daily Energy Bear 3X Shares: Russell 1000 Energy

(FAZ) Daily Financial Bear 3X Shares: Russell 1000 Financial Services

(DRV) Daily Real Estate Bear 3X Shares: MSCI U.S. REIT Index

(TYP) Daily Technology Bear 3X Shares: Russell 1000 Technology Index

(DPK) Daily Developed Markets Bear 3X Shares: MSCI EAFE Indes

(EDZ) Daily Emerging Markets Bear 3X Shares: MSCI Emerging Markets Index

(TYO) Daily 10-Year Treasury Bear 3X Shares: NYSE ARCA Current 10 Year U.S. Treasury Index

(TMV) Daily 30-Year Treasury Bear 3X Shares: NYSE ARCA Current 30-Year U.S. Treasury Index

As is the case with any sophisticated financial product, you must educate yourself and come armed with knowledge in order to be successful. A careful review of prospectuses, warnings, and fund components and a thorough understanding of the risks are prerequisites before wading into these challenging waters.

Leveraged Exchange Traded Funds can be powerful tools in the right hands. However, to be successful with these ETFs, you must know what you're doing because as Warren Buffett so famously has said, "When you combine ignorance and leverage, you get some pretty interesting results."[2]

ACTIVELY MANAGED EXCHANGE TRADED FUNDS

Actively managed ETFs are a relatively new development that combines the features of an ETF with active management.

As we've discussed, ETFs in their basic form track an underlying index with no attempt at active management and so should perform like the index performs. An actively managed ETF will have the assets of the fund actively managed by a trader or advisor who will be attempting to outperform its underlying index.

Major providers like State Street Global, Vanguard, and Claymore, among others, are all participating in this growing field. The idea here is to bring to ETFs the active management feature of mutual funds.

CURRENCY EXCHANGE TRADED FUNDS AND EXCHANGE TRADED NOTES

Currency ETFs and ETNs are designed to offer investors exposure to various foreign currency markets that haven't previously been available outside of futures contracts.

One of the primary providers of currency ETFs is Rydex Investments which offers a group of funds called Currency Shares. Currency Shares offers exposure to the following currencies:

(FXA): Currency Shares Australian Dollar Trust
(FXB): Currency Shares British Pound Sterling Trust
(FXC): Currency Shares Canadian Dollar Trust
(FXE): Currency Shares Eurodollar
(FXY): Currency Shares Japanese Yen
(FXM): Currency Shares Mexican Peso Trust
(XRU): Currency Shares Russian Ruble
(FXS): Currency Shares Swedish Krona
(FXF): Currency Shares Swiss Franc Trust

Other possibilities for exposure to the currency market are offered by ProShares Funds that offer both leveraged long and short currency ETFs:

(ULE): Ultra Euro: Euro/U.S. Dollar
(YCL): Ultra Japanese Yen: Japanese Yen/U.S. Dollar
(EUO): Ultra Short Euro: Euro/U.S. Dollar
(YCS): Ultra Short Yen: Japanese Yen/ U.S. Dollar

A wide variety of ETFs in subindex and subsectors are also available, including sub sectors like coal, nuclear energy, solar energy, Brazilian real estate as well as smaller country funds like Israel and Peru. The list of these would make up a book of its own and new entries come along on a regular basis.

CONCLUSION

So you can see that the ETF universe is ever expanding and offers investors and traders a virtually limitless array of investment choices and opportunities. And this discussion barely scratched the surface of the different opportunities available. Aside from the current variety of funds in the market, new ones are being added almost every day and it could be just about a full-time job to keep up with the new funds arriving and old ones closing.

In the Resources Section, I've provided a list of major ETF providers so you can research this overwhelming list on your own to find areas of particular interest.*

---

*Note: All ETF providers and names mentioned in this chapter are registered trademarks of the specific corporation and the author has no affiliation with any of these entities and no recommendations as to suitability or performance is made or to be implied. This list is for informational purposes only.

PART III

Sector Rotation: What It Is and Why It Works

The "smart money" long ago discovered the power of sector rotation trading strategies to profit in any market environment regardless of whether the general indexes were going up, down or sideways.

Interestingly—and perhaps not surprisingly—sector rotation strategies have not been widely embraced by most retail investors, and even recently, with the advent of an almost unlimited number of Exchange Traded Funds, sector rotation is still not a widely employed trading strategy.

Traditional sector rotation philosophy has been tied to various stages of the economic cycle, but since the onset of The Great Recession, a new type of sector rotation has been in play in the markets, as well.

In this section, we'll delve into traditional sector rotation philosophy, what it is, how it works, and why it works during various periods of the economic cycle.

We'll discuss how and when various sectors take the lead under normal economic conditions and then we'll take a close look at how The Great Recession and the concurrent period of extreme market stress have changed the face of sector rotation, possibly forever.

CHAPTER 6

Sector Rotation—The Traditional View

T he United States economy goes through clearly defined business cycles that resemble peaks and valleys and that are formally known as
periods of recession or expansion. Within these business cycles are
several specific stages and in each stage, particular sectors tend to be the
leaders while others tend to lag general market performance.

As market leadership shifts from one sector to another, a good sector
rotation trading system searches for profits by identifying market leaders
and so can oftentimes outperform the general indexes regardless of the
conditions the general markets are experiencing.

THERE'S ALWAYS A BULL MARKET SOMEWHERE

"There's always a bull market somewhere" is a well worn but very true
aphorism. No matter what "the market" is doing, up, down, or sideways,
there really is always a bull market somewhere and sector rotation trading strategies are designed to find and exploit these "mini-bull" or "stealth"
bull markets.

It's a lot easier task during bull market years when the major indexes
and subsectors are all in upswings. During these periods the challenge is to
make more money than the averages by focusing on the strongest sectors,
and there are well-defined ways to do this.

It's a little tougher to "beat the market" during bear market years because many subsectors are also in decline along with the general indexes,

but surprisingly, one can even profit in bear market years because subsectors that are rising can always be found.

On top of that possibility is the new opportunity provided by the inverse Exchange Traded Funds that let you make money as the underlying index or sector declines. As we discussed earlier, these ETFs increase in value as the underlying index declines and so, effectively, you're turning a bear market into a bull by "shorting" with an inverse Exchange Traded Fund.

Even during the dark years of 2008 when most investors took double digit losses approaching or even exceeding −50 percent, there were sectors producing profits for investors who could identify their performance. With a major meltdown like 2008, the best opportunities are usually found on the "short" side of the market, naturally, and several Exchange Traded Funds offered the opportunity to profit from the decline.

Here are examples of specific results during 2008 and why sector rotation can supercharge your portfolio.

PSQ: Short QQQ ProShares: +51.5 percent
SH: Short S&P 500 ProShares +37.5 percent
DOG: Short Dow 30 ProShares: +29.8 percent

But other asset classes could have provided shelter, as well:

TLT: Barclay's 20 Year Bond Fund: +28.3 percent
FXY: Currency Shares Japanese Yen Trust: +22.9 percent
GLD: SPDR Gold Trust: +4.9 percent
UUP: PowerShares Bullish Dollar Index: +4.2 percent

In 2009, the big story was the explosive rally that began in March. Through mid-November, 2009, the S&P 500 was up +21 percent but even more impressive gains were achieved in sectors like Brazil, which gained +114 percent, Vietnam +68 percent, Emerging Markets Index +64 percent, and Silver gaining +53 percent.

These kinds of potential returns are why "the smart money" has gravitated towards sector rotation, because there isn't just "one market" but rather a wide variety of "sub-markets," some of which will always be in significant uptrends and outperforming the general indexes. Since sector rotation trading strategies allow the investor to identify and profit from sectors that are outperforming the general market, they make an obviously valuable addition to any portfolio.

Today's investment options are numerous. The incredible range of choice mandates careful consideration and selection. Like other investment strategies, sector rotation investing requires study, practice, and discipline, but when applied correctly offers the potential to enhance one's overall returns.

NINE BASIC SECTORS

Most discussions of sector rotation focus on the nine industry sectors tracked by the Select Sector SPDR Series of Exchange Traded Funds that cover the basic industry groups in the S&P 500.

1. Technology (XLK)
2. Industrials (XLI)
3. Consumer Discretionary (XLY)
4. Materials (XLB)
5. Energy (XLE)
6. Consumer Staples (XLP)
7. Health Care (XLV)
8. Utilities (XLU)
9. Financial (XLF)

These nine sectors are represented by their corresponding Exchange Traded Funds (symbols in parentheses) and are highly liquid and actively traded issues. In Figure 6.1 we see the sector rotation model that matches up the sectors with the corresponding economic cycle.

So the theory is pretty simple. All you have to do is figure out which stage of the economic cycle you're in and then buy those sectors that are typically the leaders during that phase.

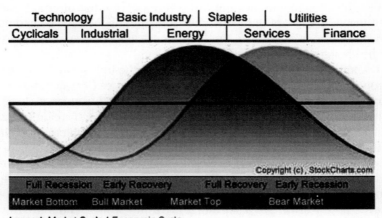

FIGURE 6.1 Sector Rotation Model
Chart courtesy StockCharts.com

Looking at Figure 6.1 and starting from the left with full recession, we can see that if we're following this theory, we should be focusing on Technology and Cyclical, and, in fact, those two sectors have performed much more powerfully as The Great Recession draws to a close.

Then in the early recovery stage we should switch to Industrials and Energy and as 2010 draws to a close we are seeing substantial strength in both of those areas. And as the recovery continues, a good sector rotation plan might be to switch to Staples, Services, and then finally Utilities and Finance as the next recession and bear market begin.

WILL THIS TIME BE DIFFERENT?

The theory of sector rotation works well in a normal business cycle. However everyone would agree that The Great Recession was anything but a normal business cycle recession and so it would make sense that the recovery might also differ from "normal" and so sector rotation might be different as well.

There are several reasons for this. First of all, we have experienced unprecedented levels of government intervention into all corners of the American free enterprise system. As I write this, the government effectively runs the financial and insurance sectors, the automotive sector, and as the Obama Administration's health care reform bill moves through Congress, governmental tentacles are reaching far into the health care sector, as well.

Furthermore, unlike other recessions, we have seen the consumer, who comprises 70 percent of the U.S. economy, take enormous hits to his net worth and sense of security through the popping of the stock market bubble, the housing bubble, and the severe contraction of credit that has taken place. It appears that consumer spending might have been changed forever and if that's the case, then the American economy might also very well be changed forever.

Looking at individual sectors, we see that the Industrial Sector has undergone substantial change with the bankruptcies of Chrysler and General Motors and the government's involvement in those businesses along with the outsourcing of enormous manufacturing capacity to foreign countries.

The Energy Sector has been impacted by the wild fluctuations in the price of oil and here, too, we see the hand of government reaching in with talk of green energy, carbon tax credits, and climate change initiatives.

Consumer Staples is perhaps the only sector not likely to see major changes as people will still need to buy food and toilet paper and clothes, but even here we will see a shifting away from "wants" and more towards "needs" as consumers deleverage and downshift their expectations in the new world that lies ahead.

Health Care is about to undergo a dramatic change with the health care reforms moving through Congress and as the baby boom ages and puts increasing demands on this system, the face of health care is likely to undergo dramatic and permanent alteration.

Utilities are quite likely going to shift from being a defensive play to being a growth play as the country is in desperate need to upgrade and modernize its power grid. Emission standards for factories and utilities are likely to add costs and change the nature of this business as well.

And finally, the Financial Sector is a mere shadow of its former self and a totally transformed entity. Companies that have been around since the dawn of time have disappeared and the "too big to fail" group has consolidated power in a way not seen in decades. Government regulation is sweeping through this sector from executive compensation to new regulations to prevent another meltdown like the 2007–2008 calamities, and bank failures will continue for years as bad credit defaults and commercial real estate loans and credit card and residential loans are written off.

It's not too strong to say that a financial tsunami has swept across the world and new rules for lending, weakened banks, weakened consumers, and toxic assets, will take years of cleanup before we see any semblance of normal. All of this is to say that the standard sector rotation model of the past might not be as effective this time around, and investors will have to adjust to these macro changes if they expect to be successful in the coming environment.

The overriding danger for the U.S. economy is the health of the U.S. consumer, who, as we mentioned, makes up 70 percent of the U.S. economy. Every day there are anecdotal reports of changes in spending habits, changes in saving habits, a move to smaller cars and smaller homes and smaller vacations, and if these changes are permanent, companies and investors will have to undergo serious readjustments to this new world.

The later chapters of this book will address what I see as "super sectors" in the decade ahead and where the most opportunities will very likely be found. Due to the rapidly changing nature of financial markets, it's quite possible that the sector rotation of tomorrow will be quite unlike the sector rotation of yesterday.

THE BUSINESS CYCLE HAS NOT BEEN REPEALED

However, even with the far-reaching changes we've just experienced, I believe that the business cycle has not been repealed. There will always be recessions in which we see Gross Domestic Product declining for at least two quarters which leads to rising unemployment and declining manufacturing, sales, and earnings.

Somewhere during the recession a bottom is reached where business activity slows further and incomes decline. People are cutting back on their spending and hunkering down and have no confidence in the future or the economy.

As this period wears on, inventories are slowly depleted and people find themselves having to buy cars to replace old ones, and pent-up demand for vacations and eating out starts to take over which gradually leads to recovery and expansion. The first signs of recovery are slowing job losses followed by hiring at temporary agencies, which leads to permanent hiring and job growth which, in turn, leads to higher consumer spending, more demand, and growing business activity and then a move up toward an economy operating near full capacity.

Life at the top of the business cycle is good if only we could stay there. Alas, inflation usually starts, the Fed has to raise interest rates to keep inflation in check, and that adds to the cost of doing business and leads to a slowing of growth followed by a decline in business activity and a descent back into the next recession.

WHY USE SECTOR ROTATION?

It has been widely proven in numerous studies that there are always certain sectors that have outperformed the general market. Over time, most price changes in companies' stocks are related to and dependent upon the sector they're in, so it only makes sense to have your assets deployed in top performing sectors. You could be the best stock picker who ever lived, but if your choice lies in a weak or weakening sector, all your work will very likely be for naught and your darling will most likely still underperform average companies in stronger sectors.

Beyond opportunities for outperforming "the market," sector rotation offers the opportunity for true diversification and into assets that can move in an uncorrelated fashion with the general indexes.

CONCLUSION

In this chapter we've looked at the basic tenets of traditional sector rotation and which sectors to watch for being potential leaders at various stages of the business cycle.

Exchange Traded Funds and sector rotation used together offer you the ability to focus your attention and assets towards "sub markets" that you've identified as being in significant up-trends. Beyond that advantage, a solid sector rotation plan using Exchange Traded Funds allows you to "short" the market and so effectively turn bear markets into bull markets. So no matter what the general markets are doing, there's always a bull market somewhere.

Sector rotation is like wearing the right clothes for the right season. You wouldn't go on a ski vacation dressed for Hawaii, nor would you show up on the beach in your ski parka and woolen hat. The stock market is much the same way. Every sector has its season and if you can align yourself with those seasons you can find enormous opportunities to outperform the general indexes and sidestep the wealth destruction inherent in bear markets.

CHAPTER 7

The New Science of Sector Rotation

I n Chapter 6 we touched upon the possibility that sector rotation might work a bit differently this time around because of the unprecedented nature of The Great Recession and the subsequent recovery efforts by sovereign states around the world.

Other factors are at work in the world's equity markets that are new elements that investors will have to understand in order to be successful. First is the changing nature of sectors themselves, followed by the speed with which money moves around the world and the fact that many retail investors appear to have exited the equity markets, possibly for good.

IT'S A BRAVE NEW WORLD

It's very likely that The Great Recession and the unprecedented amount of liquidity that has been pumped into our financial system could have significant effects on global equity markets in general and sector rotation, in particular, for many years to come.

The stock market rally of 2009 has been unlike anything anyone has ever seen unless you were around for the Great Depression in the 1930s. Government participation in free enterprise is at unprecedented levels and clearly has affected the way in which the capital markets operate.

I'm not a believer in conspiracy theories or outright government manipulation of the world's stock markets but there can be no question that central bank actions during 2009 have dramatically affected the action of global equities markets.

I have a good friend who's a very successful money manager who complains, rightly so, that "you can't model government intervention," and this goes for sector rotation, as well, which has taken on a remarkably different tone as the country and the world emerge from The Great Recession.

In this chapter, we're going to take a look at what I call "The New Science of Sector Rotation," and we're going to start off by taking a look at the nine basic sectors of the S&P 500 and how things might have already changed.

ARE THERE ONLY NINE SECTORS?

The traditional view of sector rotation confines itself to the nine major sectors on the S&P 500 and in my view, this interpretation is no longer accurate or even valid. The world has become a much bigger place, so to speak, and today investors have an almost unlimited number of sectors available in which to gain exposure.

Today Exchange Traded Funds offer exposure to the traditional sectors as well as all sorts of new things like Precious Metals, International, Developing Markets, Currencies, and Commodities.

In our previous discussion, it became obvious that the top performing sectors for 2008 and 2009 had little or nothing to do with the standard nine sectors usually considered by the science of sector rotation. In fact I believe that the greatest opportunities ahead will be found not in the standard nine sectors, but in new sectors that have previously been unavailable to American retail investors.

It's an exciting time and there are more opportunities than ever before for investors and traders willing to look beyond traditional boundaries and traditional asset classes.

THE VELOCITY OF MONEY AND THE INCREDIBLE DISAPPEARING INVESTOR

Ever since the violence of the bear market in 2008 and subsequent explosive rally of 2009, the very nature of the U.S. stock markets seems to have changed.

Volumes are dramatically lower than before the bear hit and it appears that many retail investors have fled the equities markets for the perceived safety of the bond market. This absence of a multitude of small investors has not only led to lower volumes but also to dramatic increases in volatility.

Market moves that used to take years to unfold now happen in months, months are compressed into days, and days into single sessions. The frequency of 1 percent or greater moves on the major indexes is at levels unseen since the Great Depression and at the time of this writing, shows no sign of letting up.

Today the New York Stock Exchange looks more and more like a commodity pit or foreign exchange market where big players can move the market seemingly at will, and increasingly it feels more like a gambling casino than a bona fide stock exchange where shares are traded based on inherent value or at least the perceived value of the underlying companies.

Also contributing to the volatility is the speed at which information travels around the world, the power and speed of the super computers running the big trading desks, and the ease of buying and selling equities and ETFs with the push of a button on your laptop or smartphone.

All of this makes for a more competitive environment and investors and traders have to adapt or be left behind.

Let's take a look at the nature of sector rotation in this new environment and at how much things have changed and how fast things are moving. We'll start our exploration by taking a look at Figure 7.1 and the ETF that tracks the oil market, the United States Oil Fund.

Taking a look at the United States Oil Fund (USO), we can see approximately a +60 percent positive move during the first half of 2008, followed by approximately a −80 percent drop through March 2009, only to be reversed to a +60 percent gain over the first 11 months of 2009.

The chart of USO in Figure 7.1 clearly demonstrates the speed and velocity of money moving in and out of this market over a very compressed time period. This velocity and volatility offer enormous opportunity for agile traders but also enormous dangers for buy and hold investors or less agile traders. Figure 7.2 shows us a view of FXI, the iShares FTSE/Xinhua China 25 Index over the same period of time:

The same type of violent price action is evident as money moved into and out of this market at a pace that surpasses anything we've seen in recent history. Figure 7.3 (see p. 60) is a picture of GLD, the SPDR Gold Trust and it, too, shows the same kind of volatility and rapid fire changes of direction.

And in the chart in Figure 7.4 (see p. 61), we see the movements of "conservative" bond fund, the 20-Year Treasury.

In traditional sector rotation philosophy, certain sectors are supposed to lead the way out of recession and one of these is Industrials, as depicted in Figure 7.5 (see p. 61).

Another perennial leader during economic recoveries is Technology and in Figure 7.6 (see p. 62) we can see how it has performed during the early days of recovery from The Great Recession, bouncing off the March lows and blasting steadily higher through the end of the year.

FIGURE 7.1   United States Oil Fund (USO)
Chart courtesy of StockCharts.com

As you would correctly expect, we've seen significant gains in these sectors with Technology gaining approximately +70 percent from its lows and Industrials climbing +80 percent from its lows.

Two late cycle sectors are Utilities and Financials and these usually don't come to life until later in a recovery, but here we see how they have fared in the early going. Figure 7.7 (see p. 62) shows us how Financials have done, which is particularly interesting, since the Financial Sector has been one of the most heavily influenced by government actions in its panic to save institutions that have been deemed "too big to fail."

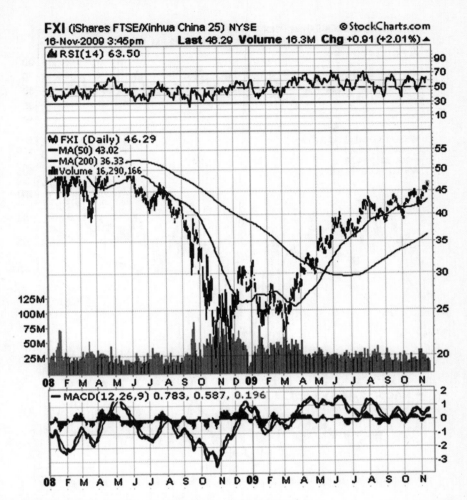

FIGURE 7.2 FXI: iShares FTSE/Xinhua China 25 Index
Chart courtesy of StockCharts.com

Supposedly a lagging sector, the Financial Sector is up an impressive +147 percent from its lows at the depths of the bear market.

In Figure 7.8 (see p. 63) we see a graphic picture of the supposedly stodgy Utility Sector and even this haven for widows and orphans has added an impressive +26 percent over the course of less than one year's market action.

Likewise, taking a look at Energy in Figure 7.9 (see p. 63), this mid-cycle leader in normal times has logged better than +50 percent gains.

FIGURE 7.3   Gold 2008–2009
Chart courtesy of StockCharts.com

Not to mention Gold's impressive performance of more than + 50 percent depicted in Figure 7.10 (see p. 64).

Looking outside the traditional nine sectors we see many examples of even more stellar returns, like Brazil gaining more than +120 percent from its March Lows in Figure 7.11 (see p. 64).

When you look at all of these charts put together, one thing becomes very clear; they all look remarkably alike. Just as nearly all asset classes were compressed and moved as one during the bear market, they have all

FIGURE 7.4 iShares 20-Year Treasury Bond (TLT)
Chart courtesy of StockCharts.com

FIGURE 7.5 Industrials Select Sector SPDR
Chart courtesy of StockCharts.com

FIGURE 7.6 Technology Select Sector SPDR
Chart courtesy of StockCharts.com

FIGURE 7.7 Financials Select SPDR
Chart courtesy of StockCharts.com

FIGURE 7.8 Utilities Select Sector SPDR
Chart courtesy of StockCharts.com

FIGURE 7.9 Energy Select Sector SPDR
Chart courtesy of StockCharts.com

FIGURE 7.10 Gold (GLD)
Chart courtesy of StockCharts.com

FIGURE 7.11 Brazil Index
Chart courtesy of StockCharts.com

FIGURE 7.12 S&P 500
Chart courtesy of StockCharts.com

become compressed and have been moving close to being one during the subsequent recovery.

So traditional sector rotation philosophy has—for the time being, at least—been overridden by the Federal Reserve and the enormous liquidity coursing through the market. Instead of a smooth cycle of leadership change and outperformance, all sectors are barreling ahead at the same time.

A quick glance at the S&P 500 chart tells us one more interesting thing in Figure 7.12.

Its rise looks a lot like the other charts but with a significant difference. It's up an impressive +21 percent over this same time period but this just puts it in the "stodgy" class of Utilities and makes it a comparative underperformer to almost every sector available to investors today.

CONCLUSION

So what can we conclude from all of this?

It does seem that we're living in a new world created by massive government intervention, unprecedented liquidity, the virtual disappearance of the retail investor from the world's equity markets, and the velocity of money moving around the world at near the speed of light.

Clearly during significant downturns, all asset classes tend to get compressed and move as one. But, perhaps unexpectedly, during subsequent upturns, traditional sector rotation gives way to most asset classes being compressed and moving as one to the upside.

But even within this unilateral upward movement, certain sectors have been leaders with outsized gains and almost all of them have beaten the general market averages.

Finally, this study makes crystal clear the fact that limiting oneself to the traditional nine sectors of sector rotation philosophy locks you out of a whole world of opportunity in alternative asset classes that have previously been unavailable to retail investors and traders.

PART IV

Trading Systems Designed to Outperform the Indexes

T he single most important decision you can make as a trader is to choose a system that is a good match for you. When I say "a good match," you must find a system that fits everything about you.

In this section we're going to take a look at three trading systems designed to outperform the indexes. These systems range in complexity from very low maintenance strategies to almost full-time jobs and so by the end of this section, you'll have a full range of options from which to choose. I'm doing this because you must find a system that is compatible with *all* of the following factors:

YOUR PERSONALITY

This is probably the single most important factor in your decision making. Are you suited for day trading or longer term trend-following systems? Do you like fast-moving, high-risk situations or a longer term and more stable environment? Do you have the discipline to stick with a program every day or do you get discouraged easily and give up quickly?

What is your risk tolerance? Can you afford to lose a lot of money or any money at all? I meet people all the time in my business who "don't want to lose any money." If that's you, then trading is definitely not for you. Active trading will automatically generate losses and you need to accept that simple, indisputable fact before ever getting started.

The only way to find out for sure about all of these things is to paper trade different styles of systems for a period of time to find one that fits you. A day trader is a substantially different animal from a long-term trend follower and if you don't find a system that fits you, you are destined to fail.

YOUR LIFESTYLE

Do you have a full time job and a family? Or are you retired and have time to sit at your computer all day and trade? This is a critical decision because if you have to get up at 4:00 AM every day and trade before you go to work or check your charts after work, I can guarantee you that you'll burn out over time and not be successful trading over the long term. You must find a system that fits with your lifestyle and time commitments.

YOUR GOALS

Before you spend one minute trading, you must determine what your goals are. Do you want to increase your net worth for retirement? Do you want to make trading a full-time career? Do you want to be a gambler and "play" the market? The answers to these questions will help determine which type of trading system you should choose.

Once you answer these questions, you'll know which types of systems could be suitable for you.

CHAPTER 8

Almost Like Buy and Hold

A s we discussed in Chapter 2, buy and hold is an almost universally accepted way to invest but one that could be fatally flawed in today's modern market environment. But the idea that you could just invest in a diversified portfolio and leave it alone is appealing because if you have a busy life, it's very likely that active trading won't fit into your schedule or not be something that you could pursue on a long-term basis.

If that sounds like you, then here's a concept that could allow you to basically buy and hold but still sidestep major bear markets that could wipe out years of gains or set you up for years of losses. Basically this a long-term trend following system based upon the S&P 500 which is considered a proxy for the U.S. stock market. The vehicle we'll use for this study is the SPY, the original ETF affectionately known as the SPYDR, since its inception in the mid-1990s.

This system is so simple that a sixth grader could do it. Although it isn't perfect, as no system is, we'll see as we step through the last few years that it's far superior to buy and hold and that success can be achieved without a lot of work or time commitment.

We'll start by taking a look at (SPY) the SPDR S&P 500 ETF that is the largest ETF in the world and considered a proxy for the U.S. stock market. Figure 8.1 is a chart of SPY from 1994 to 2009 and here we'll get a "big picture" view of the U.S. stock market over the last fifteen years.

Figure 8.1 is a weekly chart of the SPY with a 70-week moving average overlaid on top of the price action. The average line starts in 1995 and you can see how the price moves above the moving average line from 1995

FIGURE 8.1 SPY 1994–2009
Chart courtesy of StockCharts.com

through 1998 where it takes a short dip before continuing upwards to a peak in 2000.

Here we see the SPY turn and cross below the 70-week moving average at the beginning of the "tech wreck." As we move across the chart to the right, we see that the price bars stay below the 70-week moving average until mid-2003, when the bear market ended and went on a long bull market uptrend that lasted until the most recent bear market began in 2008.

In early 2008, we see SPY drop below the 70-week average and then take a waterfall plunge through the year as the bear market associated with The Great Recession dug its claws into investors around the world. The bear continued until about mid-2009 and then suddenly SPY reversed off the now famous March Lows, and in a matter of just a few months rocketed up and through the 70-week average, signaling the end of at least this leg of the bear market—in approximately June 2009.

This is interesting price action, to say the least, and so let's take a closer look at this fifteen-year period that encompassed two significant bear markets with one intervening rally and a new rally just underway. We'll take a look at this in broad terms from the viewpoint of an investor who just wants to invest on the long side in the S&P 500 with the goal of maximizing upside gains and minimizing downside losses.

In broad terms we can see an investor, following this simple system, would have ridden a bull market wave from the low $40s in 1995 on the

SPY up to roughly the mid $120s when he would have gone to cash in 2001. He would have stayed in cash until 2003 when we would have again reentered the market in the high $80s. At that point we would have stayed long until 2008 and then stepped to the sidelines at about $135. We would have stayed in cash until mid-2009 where our buy signal would have us reenter the market at about $100 per share.

So by following this simple system, it looks like we would have captured gains of approximately 200 percent between 1995 and 2001, 50 percent between 2003 and 2008 and 10 percent between mid and late 2009 for a total of 260 percent between 1995 and 2009, or roughly a 14-year period.

During this same period, a buy and hold investor would have ridden through two bear markets (if he could have psychologically withstood the declines) for a gain of about 145 percent. Clearly just being able to sidestep major bear markets would go a long way to improving your portfolio performance and this doesn't count a guy who could "go short" during the declines.

All of these benefits could have been reaped just by following a very simple system on a weekly basis and just by using the S&P 500 index and nothing else fancy or complicated. It's not written anywhere that trading has to be fancy or complicated or that you need a super computer to be a success. But you do need a system and be able to apply some discipline to your program to make it work.

BUT IT'S NOT THAT EASY

Of course it couldn't be that easy, because if it was, everyone would be doing it. But "the catch" isn't too onerous. And "the catch" is that like in every trend-following system there are going to be periods where you get whipsawed as the price moves around the moving average during directional changes in the market.

However, by using a long-term weekly average, we can smooth out the trading action and eliminate most, but not all, of the whipsaws.

Here's a summary of the total trading action between July 1994 and November 2009, a nearly $15\frac{1}{2}$ year period.

Total Trades: 9
Winners: 4
Losers: 4
Breakeven: 1
Largest Loser: −4.0 percent
Largest Winner: +109.3 percent
Total Gain: +192.9 percent

CUT YOUR LOSSES AND LET YOUR WINNERS RUN

Over the course of the last few pages, we've seen a great example of how to cut your losses and let your winners run.

By the way, the SPY over the same period for a buy and hold investor gained 145 percent and so this simple system added more than +45 percent in gains over buy and hold.

But how many investors were able to withstand the drawdowns of the Tech Wreck and the Bear Market of 2008 without just throwing in the towel or doing what they do so well, buy high and sell low? Not to mention that between 1999 and 2009, the S&P has generated a negative rate of return and many people have just given up altogether.

The Last Ten Years No one can argue with the fact that the last ten years—the period from 1999 to 2009—have not been kind to investors, and in Figure 8.2 we can see the ugly reality of the second worst decade in stock market history.

The SPY has been negative for a full ten years. Many market analysts suggest that the rally from 2003–2007 was nothing more than a bear market rally rather than a bull market, but for investors in today's short-term

FIGURE 8.2 SPY 1999–2009
Chart courtesy of StockCharts.com

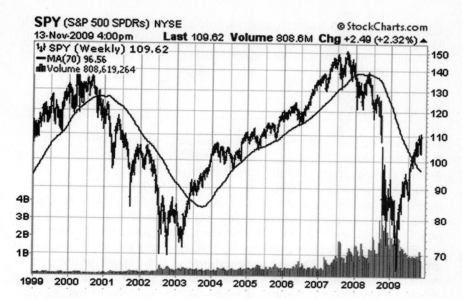

FIGURE 8.3 SPY 1999–2009 SPY with 70-Week Moving Average Overlay
Chart courtesy of StockCharts.com

memory world, a loss of a full decade is devastating, particularly for people approaching retirement, as many baby boomers are today.

Figure 8.3 is the SPY for the full decade with the 70-Week Moving Average overlaid for reference.

Just by buying when SPY moved above the 70-Week Moving Average and selling when it declined below the average, we would have caught the rebound coming off the Tech Wreck and then subsequently missed the bear market of 2008, giving us returns of approximately +60 percent over the last ten years compared to a loss of approximately −27 percent for buy and hold.

"ALMOST LIKE BUY AND HOLD" TRADING RULES

Here are the rules, which are so simple that a sixth grader could do it.

- Track the weekly closing price of the SPY.
- Overlay the 70-Week Simple Moving Average.
- When the weekly price crosses above the moving average, buy the SPY.
- When the weekly price crosses below the moving average, sell the SPY and go to cash.

More advanced traders/investors could "short" the SPY during "sell" signals or in today's world could use (SH) the ProShares Short S&P 500 Exchange Traded Fund to seek profits during market declines.

CONCLUSION

The preceding discussion is purely hypothetical because I hadn't developed this system during the time period indicated. Also it's based on tracking weekly closing prices and the actual daily price that trades would have been made would very likely have been slightly different than depicted in this discussion. Also we didn't consider dividends, taxes, or trading costs. However, this discussion should demonstrate that just by sidestepping large declines, one can still "beat the market" and beat buy and hold.

Furthermore, gains would have been significantly amplified by a trader/investor shorting the market by going short the SPY or perhaps using an inverse ETF during the downswings. The two bear markets alone generated significant interim double-digit declines which would have presented enormous potential trading opportunities on the short side.

I only wish someone would have told me about this a long time ago. If I had known about this in 1994, I would have avoided a lot of heartache, losses, and sleepless nights and the system I call "Almost Like Buy and Hold" would literally have been a game changer in terms of my financial life and security.

It's a simple system that requires very little attention to execute successfully. All it takes is just a few minutes a week and, as I mentioned, the returns could be even greater for the more sophisticated investor/trader who is willing and able to put a little more time and expertise into this method and "short" the market as well as go long.

Overall, however, it's easy to see how "Almost Like Buy and Hold" really is almost like buy and hold, but offers the potential for better risk-adjusted returns, smaller drawdowns, lower overall risk, and lots of nights with better sleep.

CHAPTER 9

The Simple Trading System

I n this chapter, we'll take a look at another simple system based on a long-term indicator that also is very easy to use and takes almost no time to manage. I call this one "The Simple Trading System" because it really is simple to use and takes virtually no time to follow. This one you have to look at on a daily basis, but only for a moment, and then you'll know instantly if any changes to your positions are needed.

Like the previous system, "Almost Like Buy and Hold," in this discussion, we'll just track the SPY over a period of years. But this time instead of using a 70-week moving average, we'll use support and resistance lines on point and figure charts.

I've been a student of Point and Figure Charting for some time and it's one of the oldest charting systems around, used by Charles Dow and in wide use long before the advent of computers and today's sophisticated charting packages. Still, though, it's a very valid charting methodology and what I like about it is that it takes all "the noise" out of the market.

We'll get into Point and Figure Charting in greater detail later in our discussion, but Figure 9.1 shows what a basic point and figure chart looks like.

Figure 9.1 is a basic chart and the columns of Xs represent times when demand is in control and prices are rising, and the Os represent times when supply is in control and prices are falling.

The two diagonal lines are known as Bullish Support and Bearish Resistance and you can see their labeling in Figure 9.1. The descending line is known as Bearish Resistance and the ascending line is labeled Bullish Support. On a regular chart these would be comparable to long-term moving

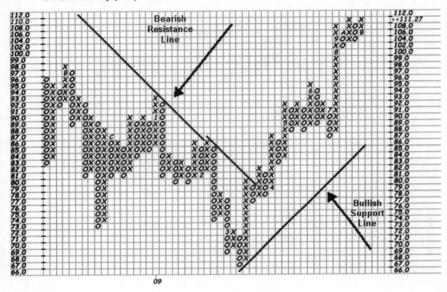

FIGURE 9.1   SPY Point and Figure Chart 2008–2009
Chart courtesy of StockCharts.com

averages and are used to depict trend changes. When prices are above the Bullish Support Line, the market is in an uptrend and when they're below the declining Bearish Resistance Line, the market is in a downtrend.

You'll notice that the Bullish Support and Bearish Resistance lines are always drawn at a 45 degree angle and so form a constant pattern of rising or declining prices.

By way of orientation, the SPY in Figure 9.1 had been in a downtrend throughout 2008 and 2009 until the column of Xs moved up through the rising diagonal Bearish Resistance line at approximately $80. At that point, the ascending Bullish Support Line was drawn from the low point of Os at approximately $67 and at a 45 degree angle up and to the right. As long as the column of Xs stays above this line, we can consider the market to be in an uptrend.

So SPY was on a trend "sell" signal when below the declining diagonal line and then shifted to a trend "buy" signal when it crossed up through the Bearish Resistance Line and continued its climb up and to the right. Figure 9.2 gives us the big picture view of the price action of SPY between 2003 and 2009.

Again, the columns of Xs indicate when demand dominates market action and the Os represent times when supply or distribution is the name of the game. In this chart you can clearly see the patterns of bull and bear markets as the columns rise, making higher highs and higher lows during bull markets above the Bullish Support Lines and fall in a series of lower highs and lower lows during bear markets.

There are several different ways to trade with point and figure charts, but to discuss "The Simple System," we're just going to focus on the crossover from bull to bear markets as represented by the columns crossing over the support and resistance lines from bull market to bear market. On a regular chart this system would be similar to trading the well-known 200-day moving average but with a lot less noise and fewer whipsaws due to the way these lines are constructed.

Over the course of the past six years as depicted in Figure 9.2, we can see the Tech Wreck coming to an end in 2003 with the start of the ascending

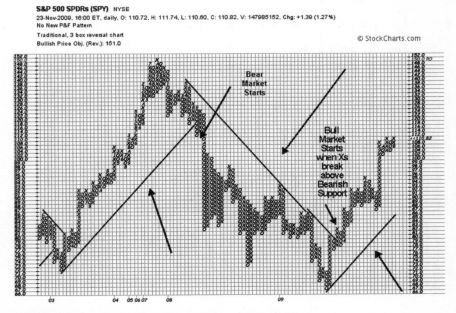

FIGURE 9.2 SPY Point and Figure Chart 2003–2009
Chart courtesy of StockCharts.com

Bullish Support Line and we can see the bull market continue until early 2008 when the trend changes and the line turns south to mark the beginning of the 2008–2009 bull market.

Time passes and then we can see the historic March rally starting when the column of Xs penetrates the Bearish Resistance Line on the way up and continues in bull market status to the time of this writing in late November 2009.

For greater clarity, let's zoom in on the crossover points, starting with Figure 9.3.

In Figure 9.3 we see the 2002 bear market coming to an end when the column of Xs pierces the Bearish Resistance line for the first time at $82.00 in mid-2002. The price climbs for a time but then right at the beginning of 2003 penetrates back below the Bullish Support line at $76. Then in the column of Xs with the "4" at the bottom, representing the month of April, the column of Xs again penetrates the Bearish Resistance Line at $82 and the bull market is underway in earnest through the rest of 2003.

The bull market continues through the end of 2004 as seen in Figure 9.4. Figure 9.5 gives us a "big picture" look from 2003 through 2007.

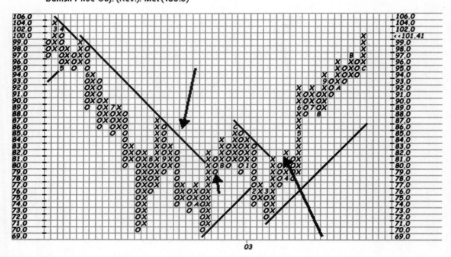

FIGURE 9.3   SPY Point and Figure Chart ending December 2003
Chart courtesy of StockCharts.com

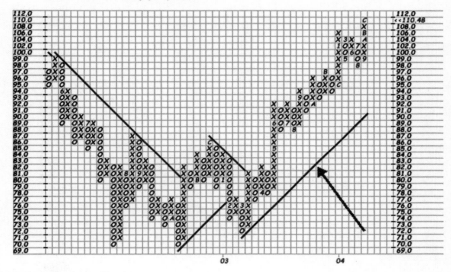

S&P 500 SPDRs (SPY) NYSE
31-Dec, 16:00 ET, daily, O: 110.877, H: 111.206, L: 110.419, C: 110.483, V: 31.3M, Chg: -0.238
P&F Pattern Double Top Breakout on 04-Nov-2004
Traditional, 3 box reversal chart
Prelim. Bullish Price Obj. (Rev.): 135.0

© StockCharts.com

FIGURE 9.4 SPY 2004
Chart courtesy of StockCharts.com

Figure 9.6 brings us into late 2008 where the trend makes a distinct change.

The trend change is clearly depicted in Figure 9.6 where we see the columns switch to Os and a break of the Bullish Support Line at $116 and the beginning of the bear market in early 2008.

The bear market continues through 2008 in Figure 9.7 (see p. 82) with the columns of Xs and Os making lower highs and lower lows as they descend beneath the Bearish Resistance Line.

The historic March 2009 lows are represented by the lowest column of Os and then the chart confirms the major trend change in June 2009, when the rising column of Xs crosses above Bearish Resistance Line at $80, signaling a "buy" signal.

Figure 9.8 (see p. 83) gives us a close-up look at the trend change and the subsequent rally through the last half of 2009.

And the bull market continues up to $110 in late November 2009 as seen in Figure 9.8.

S&P 500 SPDRs (SPY) NYSE
31-Dec, 16:00 ET, daily, O: 141.944, H: 142.432, L: 140.941, C: 141.259, V: 111.9M, Chg: -0.878
No New P&F Pattern

Traditional, 3 box reversal chart
Bullish Price Obj. (Rev.): Met (141.0)

© StockCharts.com

FIGURE 9.5 SPY 2003-2007
Chart courtesy of StockCharts.com

A summary of the trading action over these years using just the Bullish Support and Bearish Resistance Lines looks like this:

Buy Signal: 2003:	$82		
Sell Signal: 2003:	$76	−$6.00	−7.3%
Buy Signal: 2003:	$82		
Sell Signal: 2008:	$116	+$34.00	+41.5%
Buy Signal: 2009:	$80		
Continuing Buy			
11/23/09:	$110	+$30	+37.5%

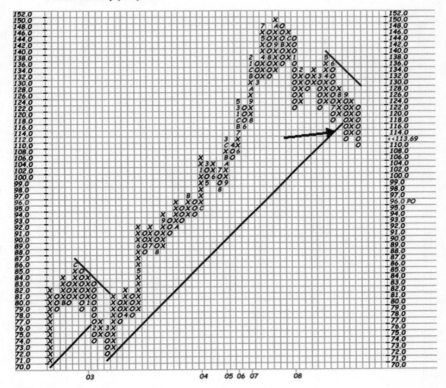

FIGURE 9.6 SPY Chart Ending September 2008
Chart courtesy of StockCharts.com

The net result on the long side only is a total of 3 trades for a net gain of $70/share or +71 percent over the course of nearly seven years. Over the same period, the SPY had a net gain of +25 percent and suffered through the gut-wrenching bear market of 2008–2009.

And this example doesn't include the opportunities presented on the "short" side if an advance investor/trader would have sold short the SPY instead of going to cash during downturns. This trader would have lost $6.00 in the 2003 whipsaw but then made an additional gain of $36 during the sell signal of the 2008–2009 Bear Market. The net extra percentage gain by going short would have been approximately an additional +23 percent for a total of +94 percent over the course of the period.

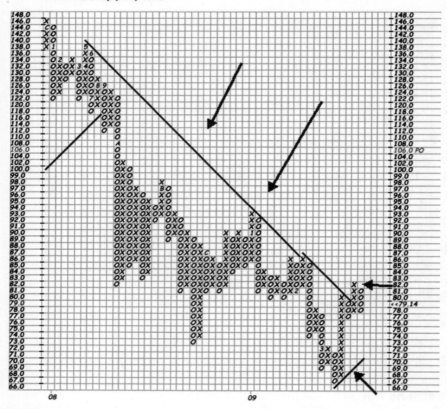

S&P 500 SPDRs (SPY) NYSE
31-Mar, 16:00 ET, daily, O: 79.183, H: 80.695, L: 78.675, C: 79.143, V: 365.8M, Chg: +0.727
No New P&F Pattern

Traditional, 3 box reversal chart
Bullish Price Obj. (Rev.): 107.0

© StockCharts.com

FIGURE 9.7   SPY Point and Figure Ending March 2009
Chart courtesy of StockCharts.com

CONCLUSION

The discussion throughout this chapter is purely hypothetical because I hadn't developed this system during the time period indicated. Also, the entry and exit prices might be slightly different based on when a trader/investor actually entered when the columns of Xs and Os penetrated the Bullish Support or Bearish Resistance Lines.

The columns represent the price range for that day and so an end of day trader would have a different fill price than a day trader or someone who

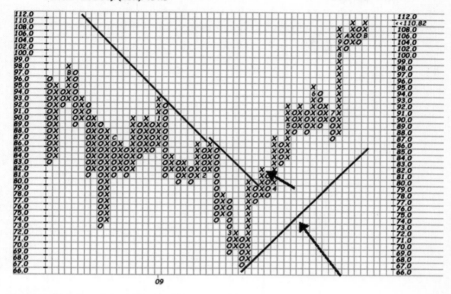

FIGURE 9.8 SPY ending November 2009
Chart courtesy of StockCharts.com

just chose to monitor this on a weekly basis. And the discussion doesn't include dividends, taxes, or trading costs. However, this discussion should demonstrate that just by sidestepping large declines, one can still "beat the market" and beat buy and hold.

Furthermore, gains would have been significantly amplified by a trader/investor shorting the market or perhaps using an inverse ETF during downswings in the SPY. The 2008 Bear Market alone generated a significant interim double-digit decline which would have presented an enormous potential trading opportunity on the short side.

This is a very simple system that requires very little work but manages to catch the big, macro trends in the market and keep you out of harm's way during declines while catching most of the upside. It will never get you in at the bottom or out at the top but it does consistently catch the meat of the rallies and sidesteps the most brutal part of the declines, thus helping to preserve capital during downtimes and grow wealth during up periods in the markets. Mostly, however, it demystifies the action of the markets and gives you a precise picture of where the market is and what its current mode is. That alone is worth a lot during confusing times like the ones in which we live.

As with the "Almost Like Buy and Hold System," "The Simple System" offers the opportunity to seek better risk-adjusted returns, smaller draw-downs, and lower overall risk by sidestepping major downturns.

CHAPTER 10

The Golden Crossover Trading System

T his chapter will look at "The Golden Crossover Trading System," another simple trading system that anyone can use. Unlike the previous two systems, "The Golden Crossover Trading System" uses a widely known combination of moving averages, the 50-Day Simple Moving Average and the 200-Day Moving Average.

Many studies have been done on various permutations of this system using different lengths of moving averages and both simple and exponential versions. In almost all cases, these have proven to outperform buy and hold with less risk because much of the time is spent in the safety of Treasury bills or cash.

More aggressive investors can also "short" the market when the "golden crossover" turns into a "death crossover," which happens when the shorter average crosses below the longer and generates a "sell" signal.

We're going to take a quick look at how these averages performed during the Bear Market of 2008 and subsequent recovery in 2009, starting with Figure 10.1, where we see the price action of SPY during 2007 through 2009.

The chart in Figure 10.1 covers the SPY from late 2007 through November 2009, and we can see the dotted line that represents the 50-Day Moving Average and the solid line that represents the 200-Day Moving Average moving along with the changes in price over this two-year period.

In late 2007, seen toward the far left of the chart, the 50-Day Simple Moving Average crossed below the 200-Day Average, indicating a sell

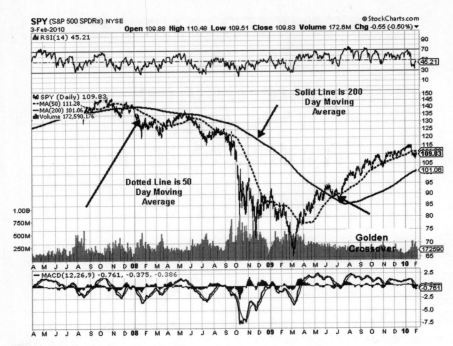

FIGURE 10.1 SPY Moving Average Crossover 2007–2009
Chart courtesy of StockCharts.com

signal, and that it was time to step aside or go short. And the 50-Day Average stayed below the 200-Day Moving Average all the way until late June, 2009, when the shorter average crossed back above the longer average and flashed a buy signal.

What could be simpler than that?

Of course it's never that easy, but this overview shows how one could have sidestepped the bear market at about the $140 level on the SPY and reentered at about $90, missing a decline of more than −35 percent. And as we've seen before, a more advanced investor/trader could have shorted the SPY at approximately $140 and then reentered on the long side at approximately $90, making a $50 profit of +35 percent while everyone else around him or her was losing money.

In the chart in Figure 10.2 we take a closer look at the crossover in 2008, and in Figure 10.3 we see what all of 2009 looked like as prices and both moving averages climbed up and to the right.

FIGURE 10.2 SPY 2007–2008
Chart courtesy of StockCharts.com

FIGURE 10.3 SPY 2009 The Golden Crossover
Chart courtesy of StockCharts.com

FIGURE 10.4 SPY 1999–2003 The Golden Crossover
Chart courtesy of StockCharts.com

So it's clear from these displays that the bear market could have easily been avoided and the subsequent rebound could have been caught just by following the signals of "The Golden Crossover."

Going back to the Tech Wreck of 2000–2003 in Figure 10.4, we see the same phenomenon taking place where "The Golden Crossover" took a short position at the top of the decline and then went long as prices started to recover in the spring of 2003.

In Figure 10.5 we see how it performed during the Bull Market of 2003–2007, and again with just one whipsaw in 2004, it kept to the long side of the market for the entire ride up over that four-year period.

Figure 10.6 gives a picture of the whole ten-year period with the 50-Day Moving Average depicted by the dotted line and the 200-Day Moving Average depicted by the solid line. Again, over the entire period when everyone else was breaking even through the pain of two bear markets, people who followed this "Golden Crossover" made just a minimal number of trades and significantly improved their risk-adjusted returns.

FIGURE 10.5 2003–2007 The Golden Crossover
Chart courtesy of StockCharts.com

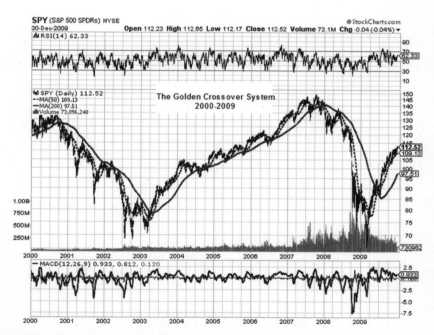

FIGURE 10.6 2000–2009 The Golden Crossover
Chart courtesy of StockCharts.com

CONCLUSION

This discussion, although hypothetical, highlights the fact that trading doesn't have to be complicated, mystical, or mysterious to be successful.

Gains were made on the upside and losses avoided on the downside and sophisticated investors again would have had the opportunity to enhance their returns by using "short" positions during market declines. This is another very simple system that requires very little work but manages to catch the big, macro trends in the market and keep you out of harm's way during declines while catching most of the upside.

Mostly, however, each of these simple systems help demystify market action and adds clarity so that you can make decisions based on reliable indicators instead of "hot tips" from friends or trying to fathom future market directions from the financial news or television.

By following the old maxim, "the trend is your friend," you can make investing and trading decisions that have the potential for higher probability outcomes than otherwise might be possible.

PART V

The Sector Scoring System: Trading Concepts, Challenges and Conundrums

Becoming a successful trader is arguably one of the most important skills you can learn because in our world, there are two kinds of ways to make money: labor and capital.

Labor is the most common way we see; our jobs, working for a paycheck or even running your own business or profession. In all cases, you have to be present most of the time to be earning money and you're trading your time—your life—for a fixed sum of money.

Capital, on the other hand, is the power of money, and when invested correctly can possess almost magical powers if it can grow and compound and bring us ever-increasing wealth. The scope of this book is focused on how to use your capital, however much or little you might have, with the goal of growing your net worth and improving your life.

In this section, we're going to cover a lot of ground and you will learn techniques and concepts that can help you become a successful trader.

This entire program is not a "black box" or a "system," but rather it's a plan for actively trading the equities markets that can be applied to stocks,

Exchange Traded Funds, mutual funds, or a multitude of other trading vehicles. There is no right way to trade, and no wrong way, and these techniques are presented to help you study and find "your" way, to develop a methodology that works for you. You can use these concepts as a complete package or you can cherry-pick the material that relates to your situation and incorporate it into any system you're currently using.

With practice and experience, I'm very confident that you can use the information in the following chapters as the foundation for becoming a successful trader.

CHAPTER 11

The Five Signals for Entering a Trade

I n this chapter, we're going to discuss the five signals for entering a trade.

Every good technical trading system is based on some sort of signal or combination of signals. There are many, many technical signals and patterns that people watch and we're going to spend a good deal of time here discussing five signals to identify potentially profitable trades.

The idea here is to use proven techniques to identify the best trades and then give you the best chance of a positive outcome. That's why we'll be using five signals, because any one signal by itself typically gives you a 50 percent chance of success, which is good enough if you manage your losing trades correctly. But we want better than a 50 percent chance of success and that's why we use five signals, to confirm the likelihood of a profitable trade.

In a later section, we'll discuss how to use these signals in real time, but for now, we'll examine each one and how it works and what we're looking for to enter a trade.

Signal No. 1: Point and Figure Charts
Buy Signals

Many people laugh when I tell them I use Point and Figure Charts because in this day of computer programs, complicated mathematical algorithms and quant-based trading systems, this system of pattern recognition seems almost primitive and archaic. In many ways it is, but the fact is that this system works and that's why it's still in existence today, more than 100 years after it was used by Charles Dow in the 1800s and later explained in detail in Victor deVillier's book, *The Point & Figure Method of Anticipating Stock Price Movements*, published in 1933.

In a nutshell, Point and Figure charts display stock price movements but without the time element displayed. A Point and Figure Chart displays only the most significant changes in price and therefore can eliminate the "noise" or "busyness" of most types of technical trading charts. This method of charting produces a very clean chart that clearly displays buy and sell signals, trend lines, support and resistance levels, and price objectives.

Let's look at the Point and Figure Chart in Figure 11.1 and dissect its elements.

Figure 11.1 is a standard Point and Figure Chart of the Microsoft Corporation from 2002 through 2009. You can see the years plotted along the bottom of the chart and the Xs depict rising prices and the demand that is driving the markets higher while the Os depict falling prices with supply overwhelming demand and driving prices lower.

The patterns the Xs and Os form a clear picture of supply and demand for the stock we're studying. When demand is driving the market, we see a series of rising columns and when supply is the driving factor in the market, we see a series of falling columns. So rising columns represent an uptrend and declining columns represent a downtrend.

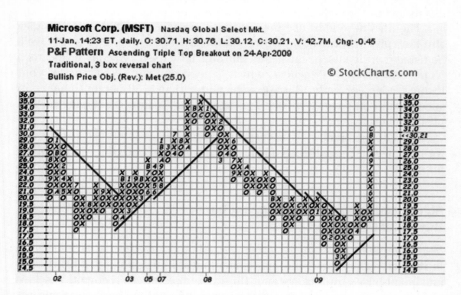

FIGURE 11.1 Microsoft Point and Figure 2002–2009
Chart courtesy of StockCharts.com

TABLE 11.1 Point and Figure Buy Signal

O				
O				
O			×	<Buy Signal
O			×	
O	×	O	×	
O	×	O	×	
O	×	O	×	
O				

Point and Figure Charts can also tell us when to buy or sell a particular security. Determining buy and sell signals is a key element of Point and Figure Charting, so let's take a look at the basic ones with which you need to be familiar. There are many variations of buy and sell signals and technicians can spend a whole career studying and perfecting their interpretation, but that simply isn't necessary to be successful using this method.

Simply put, when a column of Xs goes above the top of a previous column of Xs, a buy signal is generated, and when a column of Os descends below a previous column of Os, a sell signal is generated.

Point and Figure Buy and Sell Signals

A buy signal occurs when a column of Xs goes at least one box above a previous column of Xs as depicted in Table 11.1.

And a Sell Signal occurs when a column of Os goes below a previous column of Os as depicted in Table 11.2.

TABLE 11.2 Point and Figure Sell Signal

×				
×	O			
×	O	×		
×	O	×	O	
×	O	×	O	
×	O		O	
×			O	<Sell Signal

There are many variations of buy and sell signals but the most important thing to know about these patterns is that the larger number of boxes that are being broken above or below, the more powerful the signal is. For instance, a single box breakout is not as convincing as a quadruple box breakout.

In Figure 11.2 we look at a Triple Top Breakout on EWS, the iShares Singapore ETF.

At the top of this chart we read the caption, "P&F Pattern Triple Top Breakout," which means that this chart has just had a Triple Top Breakout and is on a buy signal. As time goes on, the pattern continues to be drawn and then we'll see "No New P&F Pattern," as depicted in Figure 11.3.

In the chart of GLD in Figure 11.3, we read in the upper left corner, "No New P&F Pattern." This means that there was no new pattern when

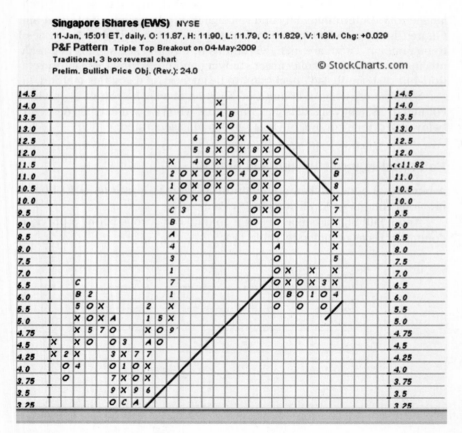

FIGURE 11.2 Point and Figure Triple Top Breakout
Chart courtesy of StockCharts.com

FIGURE 11.3 No New Point and Figure Pattern
Chart courtesy of StockCharts.com

the chart was most recently drawn. However, the notation, "Bullish Price Obj" tells us that the stock has a Bullish Price Objective and therefore is on a buy signal and that the pattern is bullish. (We'll discuss price objective in a minute.) So now we know that GLD is on a buy and has been for some unknown amount of time.

When a sell signal is generated, the chart notation will change to tell you the new pattern and the bearish status of the stock as depicted in Figure 11.4, where we see a Descending Triple Bottom Breakdown and so this security is on a sell signal with a Bearish Price Objective.

Now we know if the security we're interested in is on a buy or sell signal on our Point and Figure Chart. This is a good start, but not enough to truly give us the trading edge we need because, used alone, Point and Figure charts have about a 50 percent accuracy rate. This is enough to be profitable if you control your risk and your losses, but now we'll add in the next layers of confirmation we're looking for, to see if we have a good chance to make a profitable trade.

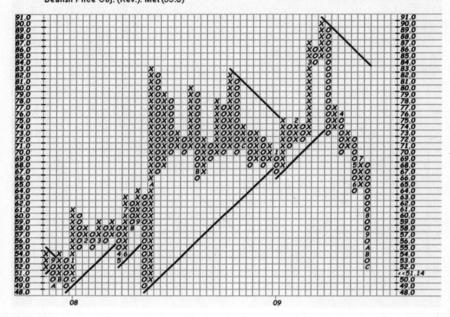

FIGURE 11.4 Descending Triple Bottom Breakdown
Chart courtesy of StockCharts.com

Signal No. 2: Point and Figure Charts: Trend and Bullish Price Objective

I'm sure you've heard the old maxim, "the trend is your friend," and indeed, even in the most volatile markets, this old saying holds true. While it is possible to trade "counter trend," that is against the trend, trading with the prevailing trend tends to lead to better outcomes.

Trend information can be used to both enter and exit trades and we'll discuss both of these methods in detail.

A quick glance at Figure 11.5 reveals prevailing trends that are immediately and easily identifiable.

Figure 11.5 shows us prevailing trends as the columns expand from left to right. Major trends are depicted by the descending or rising diagonal lines.

We also see the downward pointing arrow above the declining diagonal line known as the Bearish Resistance Line that depicts a downtrend and the

Singapore iShares (EWS) NYSE

11-Jan, 15:01 ET, daily, O: 11.87, H: 11.90, L: 11.79, C: 11.829, V: 1.8M, Chg: +0.029

P&F Pattern Triple Top Breakout on 04-May-2009

Traditional, 3 box reversal chart

Prelim. Bullish Price Obj. (Rev.): 24.0

© StockCharts.com

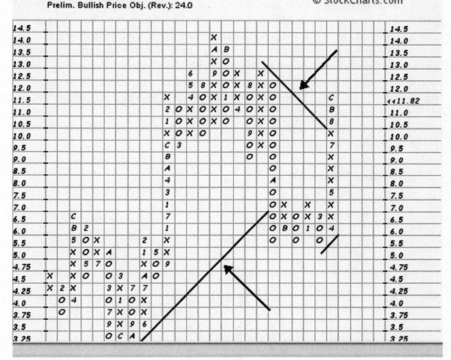

FIGURE 11.5 Singapore Point and Figure Chart
Chart courtesy of StockCharts.com

rising diagonal trend line from left to right is known as the Bullish Support Line and depicts rising trends and support levels.

Trends can also easily be picked out by observing the columns themselves and seeing a diagonal pattern of higher highs and higher lows in rising markets while a series of lower highs and lower lows depict a declining market. A quick glance from left to right in Figure 11.5 reveals an uptrend followed by a downtrend and finally in the far right column, a new uptrend that has just begun.

Point and Figure Charts can also give us major support and resistance levels. The Bullish Support Lines represent major support levels, that is, price levels where declines have previously stopped and where they could stop again.

On the other hand, Bearish Resistance Lines represent major resistance levels, levels where prices have stopped on the way up and where the price meets resistance and could meet resistance again the next time that level is reached.

As a corollary to trend information, Point and Figure Charts also give us price objectives which are determined by recent signals and are depicted by price numbers along the right-hand axis of the chart and in the top-left legend, as well. Price Objectives are not exact indicators or forecasting tools but they can give us an indication of where the price is within its trend. If price reaches the objective, typically the trend is nearing an end and one could expect a flat or declining market from there. Conversely if the current price is far from the objective, one could expect the possibility of a significant gain.

So, let's tie all this together as we look at Figure 11.6 and interpret the price action that's depicted.

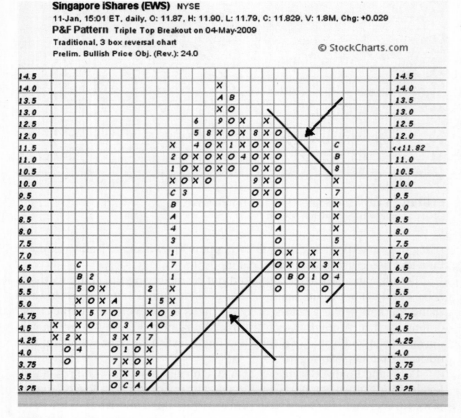

FIGURE 11.6 Point and Figure Summary
Chart courtesy of StockCharts.com

In Figure 11.6 we see that EWS is currently in a column of Xs, or rising prices, coming off the support level depicted by the Bullish Support Line below the last two columns.

At the top of the chart, we see that the Bullish Price Objective is $24 and this tells us that a buy signal is in effect and that the price objective is $24, based on recent signals and price action. With the current price at approximately $12 and with the last column of Xs having just broken through the Bearish Resistance Line, it is obvious that we're at the beginning of this trend and that upside potential could be as much as 100 percent.

We also see that the Triple Top Breakout occurred on May 4, 2009.

Our conclusion is that EWS is on a buy signal and that there could be significant upside potential without much downside risk. In other words, this looks like it could be a very favorable time to enter this trade based on what this Point and Figure Chart is telling us. And that's really all there is to interpreting a Point and Figure Chart.

Signal No. 3: Moving Average Convergence Divergence (MACD)

As I mentioned a moment ago, we're looking for confirmed buy or sell signals to give us the best chances for success. To do that, we start with the Point and Figure Buy or Sell Signal and then look at the trend for confirmation.

Sticking with our discussion of EWS, we know we have a buy signal and a positive trend, which tells us we have two long-term indicators indicating a high probability of EWS rising in price.

So now we turn to Signal No. 3, MACD, for possible further confirmation. MACD is shorthand for Moving Average Convergence Divergence which is really a mouthful but is nothing more than the combination of a trend following and momentum indicator. It has two components and we'll discuss these in some detail so you can understand how this indicator works.

MACD was invented by Gerald Appel in the 1960s and converts exponential moving averages into a momentum oscillator which gives MACD its characteristics of being both a trend and momentum indicator. The combination of moving averages and momentum allows us to study a security and determine if it's in an uptrend and if its momentum, or price velocity, is accelerating or declining.

I won't go into how MACD is built because there are hundreds, maybe thousands of variations, but the basic is the difference between a security's 12-Day and 26-Day Exponential Moving Average. Most MACD formulas add a 9-Day Exponential Moving Average to generate either a bearish or bullish trading signal.

Shorter time frames generate faster signals and longer time frames generate slower signals, depending on the trader's preference.

Moving Average Crossover

One of the most important MACD signals to me is the moving average crossover, where the MACD crosses above or below the moving average depicted in Figure 11.7.

In Figure 11.7 we see MACD displayed in the bottom panel of this chart. The two upward pointing arrows depict when MACD crosses above the moving average and the downward pointing arrow depicts a downward crossover.

Bullish moves are depicted when MACD crosses above the moving average and bearish moves, or sell signals, are depicted when MACD crosses the moving average in a downward movement.

Glancing at the main body of the chart which is the daily price action, we can see how the crossovers precede and tend to forecast changes in price action, either up or down.

Centerline Crossover

A centerline crossover is noted whenever MACD crosses over the "O" line. Moving upwards, this indicates that momentum has changed to positive

FIGURE 11.7   Moving Average Crossover
Chart courtesy of StockCharts.com

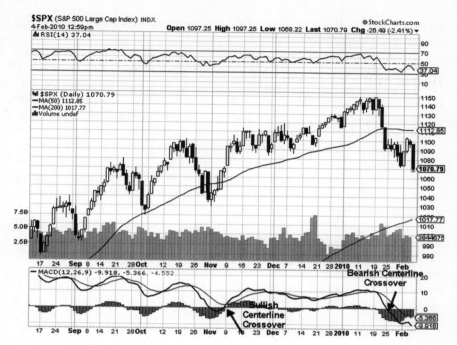

FIGURE 11.8   Centerline Crossover
Chart courtesy of StockCharts.com

and moving downward across Zero indicates that momentum has changed to negative. A shift in momentum, either positive or negative, indicates the likelihood of higher or lower prices in the near term.

The Centerline Crossover ranks as a highly reliable signal and in Figure 11.8 we see two examples of this centerline crossover when MACD crosses the "O" line.

Note in Figure 11.8 that this MACD crossover of the zero line can come with a Moving Average Crossover, as seen in the bullish cross around the 9th of November, or that it can come independently, as seen in the Bearish Crossover around January 25th. Typically a Moving Average Crossover combined with a Centerline Crossover is a very reliable signal as you have confirmation of a significant trend change taking place when both occur sequentially.

MACD Histogram

My favorite element of the MACD indicator—and the one I rely upon the most heavily—is called the histogram, the blocks below the lines themselves. The MACD histogram was developed in 1986 by Thomas Aspray and gives a pictorial depiction of a shift in momentum as well as the strength and speed of that crossover.

The histogram is a picture of the difference between the MACD and the 9-Day Exponential Moving Average. When the MACD crosses above the 9-Day Moving Average, the histogram will go above the zero line, representing a buy signal and conversely, when the MACD crosses below the 9-Day Moving Average, the histogram will start plotting below the zero line.

In Figure 11.9 we see the arrows pointing upwards at the MACD Histogram when it turns positive and downwards when it turns negative.

In Figure 11.9, we can see how the histogram expands and contracts; the taller the histogram blocks are, the more powerful the momentum up or down. And as momentum changes, the shape of the histogram changes, showing us the trend of the security's underlying momentum.

The histogram gives you a pictorial image of the motion of MACD and so it's easy to see the waxing or waning power of motion in the underlying security. If the histogram is growing taller, the momentum of the underlying security is advancing and we could expect higher prices ahead. As it shrinks towards zero we could conclude that price momentum is declining and a crossover to a "sell" signal could be coming up in the near future. The rising and falling patterns of the histogram can forecast upcoming moving average crossovers and warn us that a trend change could be in progress.

FIGURE 11.9 MACD Histogram
Chart courtesy of StockCharts.com

Used together, the MACD crossover and the histogram crossover can provide accurate indications of a security's trend and momentum. I use the histogram, MACD crossover and centerline crossover together to get a complete picture of the momentum and trend of the underlying security and have found it to be an extremely reliable, although not perfect, predictive indicator of future price action.

Daily and Weekly MACD

We've been looking at daily MACD charts but you can also consider weekly MACD to get a clear picture of the major underlying trend. My experience tells me that using Daily and Weekly MACD together gives you the best opportunity for positive confirmation and positive results of your trades.

Looking at the Weekly MACD in Figure 11.10 we see that SPY, the S&P 500 ETF, is in a long-term uptrend.

In Figure 11.10, we can see how the Weekly MACD was on a rise in July and August and then flattened out through October and November. However, the Histogram remained positive and so we can determine that price momentum has slowed but is still on a buy signal, according to the weekly MACD.

So the Weekly MACD clearly picks up and anticipates the long-term trend and traders/investors interested in holding longer-term positions can

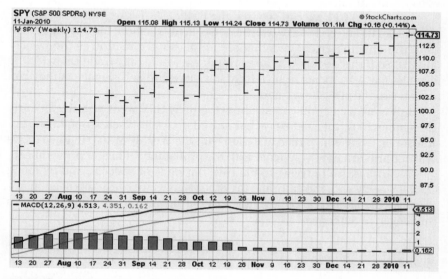

FIGURE 11.10 SPY Weekly MACD
Chart courtesy of StockCharts.com

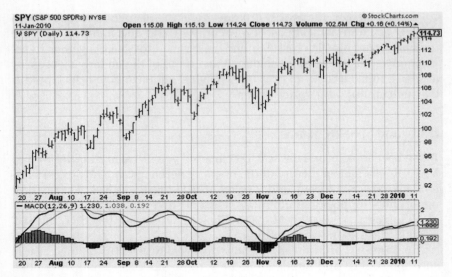

FIGURE 11.11 Daily MACD SPY June–December 2009
Chart courtesy of StockCharts.com

use these crossovers as entry and exit signals for positions in the ETF of their choice. Shorter-term traders can combine weekly with daily MACD crossovers. In Figure 11.11 we take a look at the Daily MACD for SPY.

In Figure 11.11 we can see that the Daily MACD gives much more frequent signals and so to take out the noise, in my opinion, the best approach is to use only the crossovers that are in the same direction as the weekly MACD. So if the weekly is in an uptrend, we would only trade Daily MACD signals that were positive or a buy, and disregard sell signals as they run counter to the prevailing trend.

In Figure 11.11 you can see how the daily SPY went negative in early December 2009, then sideways but stayed on a sell. Then around the 21st, it went on a buy which then matched with the Weekly MACD in Figure 11.9 and confirmed a new buy signal with the probability of higher prices ahead.

As always, we're trying to improve our odds of success, and by lining up the weekly with the daily and the other signals we see in this section, we increase the likelihood of having a positive signal and avoiding whip-saws and negative outcomes.

Summary

MACD combines momentum and trend into one indicator and can be used to predict future moves of the underlying security. Traders use MACD in all kinds of ways, but the most reliable signals come when everything is moving in the same direction.

For instance, when MACD has crossed above its moving average and has also moved above zero and the histogram is growing, you have solid indication that the security is in an uptrend. When the Daily and Weekly MACD are both going in the same direction you can consider it to be a high probability signal and that prices should rise.

Coupled with a Point and Figure Buy Signal and a positive Point and Figure trend, positive MACD readings would point to a high likelihood of rising prices ahead.

Signal No. 4: Relative Strength Index (RSI)

RSI, or Relative Strength Index, is a widely known momentum oscillator invented by J. Welles Wilder in 1978. Traders use this in different ways, but for our purposes, it is a very useful indicator for determining whether a stock is overbought or oversold, and if the security we're studying is in a generally bearish or bullish trend.

Looking at Figure 11.12, we can see that when the RSI reaches a value of 70, the stock is considered overbought and when it approaches a value of 30, it is considered oversold.

FIGURE 11.12   Russell 2000 Relative Strength
Chart courtesy of StockCharts.com

The down-pointing arrow points out a period approaching oversold at close to 30 and the up-pointing arrow is at 67.59 and approaching over-bought. Comparing to the price above in the main body of the chart, you can see how prices declined to lows in November and then climbed steadily as the RSI continued to climb to overbought levels.

Experienced traders know that if a stock is near 30 and starts rising, an excellent chance exists of a profitable trade developing, and conversely they know that as the index approaches 70, that the stock is overbought and in more dangerous territory for a decline when it turns downward.

The second use of this indicator is the trend line moving above and below the mid-point value of 50. An upward trend line passing through 50 would be bullish for the stock, while a downward trend line passing through 50 would indicate a bearish trend. This is a very simple indica-tor to use and one that gives us an excellent short-term view of the over-bought/oversold condition of a security.

The standard length used for RSI is 14 periods but you can go longer or shorter depending upon your overall orientation as a trader. Longer-term traders who like to position trade for longer periods can go to longer RSI periods, and traders with shorter-term perspectives can "speed up" the signals by using shorter-term periods.

Signal No. 5: Relative Strength

Relative strength regarding Signal No. 5 is a different interpretation of the meaning of Relative Strength we just discussed and simply looks at how a stock is performing relative to other stocks in its sector or to a specific benchmark, like the S&P 500 or Dow Jones Industrials.

This is a very important measurement for us to consider because se-curities with strong relative strength tend to rise faster than the general indexes in uptrends and tend to fall more slowly in downtrends.

Relative strength is simply calculated by dividing the price of the stock by the price of the index you want to compare it to over a specified time frame. Since we don't want to do math in public, we're fortunate that StockCharts.com allows us to very easily develop a Point and Figure Chart that depicts relative strength.

In Figure 11.13 we compare the Relative Strength of EEM, the iShares Emerging Markets Index to the S&P 500.

To get the relative strength of a security, we simply insert the security and the index we want to compare it to—like this, EEM: $SPX—and the chart magically draws itself. The ratio is highlighted by the arrow in the upper caption.

In Figure 11.13, we're comparing the relative strength of EEM, to the S&P 500, but you can use any benchmark you want, like the Dow Jones Industrials or Total Market Index.

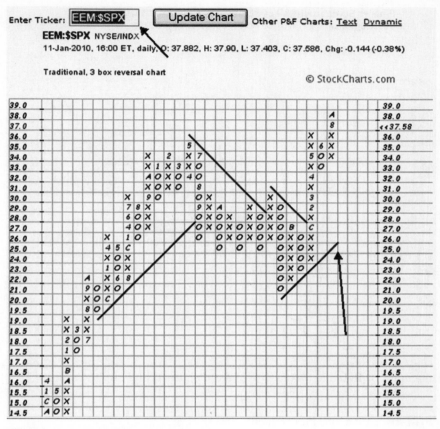

FIGURE 11.13   EEM Relative Strength
Chart courtesy of StockCharts.com

The entry format is EEM: $SPX, and in Figure 11.13, we see that EEM is in a solid upward trend against the S&P 500, well above the diagonal rising trend line and in a column of Xs.

This chart tells us that EEM has significantly stronger relative strength than the S&P 500 and has a good chance of outperforming the S&P 500 over the long term. Conversely, a security with weak relative strength compared to the S&P 500 would look like the pattern seen in Figure 11.14.

Here, it's quite easy to see that the iShares Silver Trust has been in a downtrend versus the S&P 500, well below the Bearish Resistance Line and in a declining pattern, all of which would indicate that SLV's relative strength is weak compared to the S&P 500 and so we could expect the Silver Sector to underperform the S&P 500 going forward.

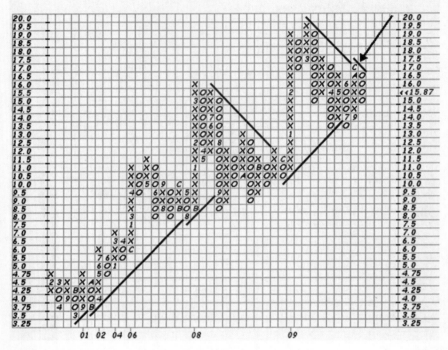

FIGURE 11.14 Relative Strength of Silver vs. SPX
Chart courtesy of StockCharts.com

Some traders use relative strength all by itself to determine what and when to buy and sell, but I've found that combining relative strength with the other indicators we've discussed gives you a great chance to find trades that present a high probability of success.

CONCLUSION

This wraps up our discussion of the Five Signals for Entering a Trade. You can see how we can drill down into any Exchange Trade Fund and get a pretty good idea of its status and potential for gain or loss as we move into the future.

Signal No. 1, Point and Figure Buy Signals, give a strong indication that the security or ETF is in a positive mode. A buy signal indicates that demand is stronger than supply and that the most likely probability is that prices will rise.

Signal No. 2, Trend and Bullish Price Objective, can confirm the Point and Figure Buy Signal and give us increased confidence in the strength of the trade we're considering. With the blocks above the Bullish Support line, we can be more confident that prices are in a long-term uptrend and the Bullish Price Objective gives us a view of what the potential gain might be.

Signal No. 3, Moving Average Convergence Divergence, MACD, takes a look at the momentum and trend of the ETF and we can use both daily and weekly readings of this indicator to confirm our notion of where the price of the ETF we're studying might be going.

Signal No. 4, RSI, tells us on a shorter term basis if now is a good time or not to enter a position. An overbought condition will usually get us into the position at a higher price than waiting for a lower RSI reading, although not always. However, entering when the ETF is oversold can oftentimes give us an edge and a lower price entry.

Signal No. 5, Relative Strength, tells us that the ETF we're studying has exhibited price action stronger than the index to which we're comparing it and so likely will outperform that index during up-moves and not decline as much during down periods.

In the next section, we'll put this basic knowledge to practical use as we compare potential trades and score them to give us a clear view of where the most profitable opportunities lie and where we would most likely have the best chance for success.

CHAPTER 12

Scoring Your Trades

I n this chapter we're going to discuss how to select what you want to trade and then how to score the possibilities you've identified to determine which potential trades have the best outcome for success.

SELECTING WHAT YOU WANT TO TRADE

This process is simpler than it sounds because today's computing power and charting packages give you the ability to designate and track an almost unlimited number of securities, Exchange Traded Funds, or mutual funds. There is a nearly unlimited universe of vehicles you can trade with these techniques and so you must decide what you want to trade.

Generally it's a good idea to start with a limited number of issues to keep things simple and easy until you become proficient at using these techniques. In my view, there is simply no need for the average investor to monitor a huge list of ETFs, stocks, or mutual funds. Big lists don't create big opportunities and only increase the workload and confusion factor. I know successful traders who limit themselves to just one index or ETF and become specialists in that area and do great. So, the old adage, "keep it simple, stupid," definitely applies to active market trading.

So for the purpose of this discussion, we're going to assume that we've selected a limited number of ETFs or mutual funds in various sectors and styles and now want to decide which ones we actually want to take positions in. (Remember that it doesn't have to be ETFs. It could also be stocks, mutual funds, or other vehicles.) After we've selected the handful of securities we want to track, we have to enter them in some sort of charting program so you can see what's actually going on with each one. There are lots of charting systems around but one that displays Point and Figure (P&F) charts—and the one we'll use for this discussion—is StockCharts.com.

StockCharts.com is a very user friendly site that does an excellent job of showing you how to build your charts with the indicators you want.

Working with a charting package is a very individual endeavor and if you are currently using a package you like, you can simply take whatever information from this book that you choose and add it to what you're already doing.

It's beyond the scope of this book to give you a complete checkout on any one charting system because each is different and each investor will use it differently, depending upon his style and personal preferences. Whichever charting program you use, it's generally a simple matter to study it and quickly become proficient in making it do what you want.

So now we'll assume you've built your Point and Figure Charts with trend line, and a basic bar chart that displays daily prices with MACD and RSI. You should also build a relative strength chart as discussed above for each security you're studying. This sounds a lot more complicated than it is, and in the end, you'll have three charts for each security you want to track.

SCORING YOUR TRADES: THE HEART OF THE SYSTEM

In this section we're going to walk through the entire process of analyzing a trade, scoring your trade against other alternative possible positions, and then lay out a checklist for every trade that you want to analyze and enter on your own. I prefer ETFs but you might want to use a number of other vehicles like individual stocks, mutual funds, currencies, or even options for your trading activities.

As we discussed above, five major signals for analyzing a trade are:

- **Signal No. 1:** Point and Figure Charts Buy Signals
- **Signal No. 2:** Point and Figure Charts Trend Information and Price Objective
- **Signal No. 3:** MACD
- **Signal No. 4:** RSI
- **Signal No. 5:** Relative Strength Comparison

Five signals are scored because this gives us the ability to score potential trades against one another and receive clarity that the potential trade does in fact have a good possibility for success. Any one signal will not be as reliable on its own, and even though it's unusual to get all five indicators with positive indications at one time, the more indicators you have in your favor, the better the chance you have for making a profitable trade.

So this becomes a simple quantitative process of applying a point value to each indicator and then putting them in a matrix to compare several potential trades at the same time.

Scoring Matrix:

Point and Figure Chart on a Buy Signal: 1 point
Point and Figure Chart Positive Trend: 1 point
Point and Figure Chart Bullish Price Objective >10 Percent: 1 point
MACD Histogram Less than 30 Daily Bars Positive: 1 Point
RSI Indicator Below 70: 1 point
Positive Relative Strength to S&P 500: 1 point

Let's take a look at a few charts to analyze this scoring system in greater detail.

Point and Figure Chart on a Buy Signal: 1 Point

In the caption of Figure 12.1, we see: "PF Pattern Triple Top Breakout." This tells us the current Point and Figure Pattern is a Triple Top Breakout and so this means EEM is on a buy signal. These charts are in color on the Internet and anytime the P&F chart has a green Point and Figure Pattern designation or a Bullish Price Objective, the chart is on a buy signal, and anytime it's a red P&F pattern and a Bearish Price Objective, it's on a sell signal.

Of course, we're only interested in Point and Figure Charts on buy signals and so you won't be spending any time analyzing charts on sell signals.

Another important consideration is when the buy signal occurred. The closer you buy to the date the signal occurred, the more likely the chance you have of making a profit because all Point and Figure signals are breakout signals and signal significant moves upwards. Therefore, the closer in time you are to the buy signal when you buy, the more likely it is that you'll capture that upward momentum. So, in our final analysis, EEM will get 1 point for its P&F Pattern Signal.

FIGURE 12.1 Point and Figure Chart
Chart courtesy of StockCharts.com

Point and Figure Chart Positive Trend: 1 Point

We've talked about the old axiom, "the trend is your friend," and another widely known slogan is, "don't fight the ticker," and both of these old sayings refer to the underlying trend of the security you're studying.

There are countless ways to measure trends that include drawing trend lines, moving averages, and mechanical indicators, but in my view, Point and Figure Charts provide one of the most accurate and easy ways to identify trends. That's because time is taken out of the chart and so the "noise" of the chart is significantly reduced, which gives you a much clearer picture of the long-term trend.

The other advantage of the Point and Figure Trend is that's it's always drawn at a 45-degree angle to the boxes and so you get a consistent view of the trend that doesn't require interpretation.

And finally, if you just look at the pattern, the highs and lows the boxes form, you can get a very clear picture of the medium-term trend at the same time the Bullish Support or Bearish Resistance lines give you the long-term trend. In Figure 12.2, you can see the price boxes well above the long-term uptrend depicted by the rising diagonal line and the arrow at the right side of the chart. You can also see a steadily rising pattern of boxes since the beginning of 2009.

So our interpretation of this trend chart tells us that the long-term trend is very strong based on its distance above the Bullish Support Line and that EEM is in a long-term up trend. For scoring purposes, just look at where the price boxes are in relation to the Bullish Support Line, that is, is the trend positive or negative, and in this case, the trend is clearly positive. Therefore, EEM gets 1 point for being in a positive trend.

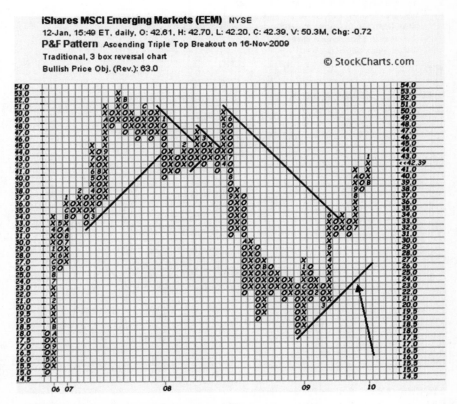

FIGURE 12.2 Point and Figure Trend Chart
Chart courtesy of StockCharts.com

Point and Figure Chart Bullish Price Objective
>10 Percent: 1 Point

Now let's take a look at Bullish Price Objective for EEM in Figure 12.3.

    The Bullish Price Objective is highlighted by the arrow in the caption of Figure 12.3 and tells us that $163 is the predicted high potential of this move based on the previous P&F columns. The Bullish Price Objective in this example is $63 compared to the closing price of $42.39. This tells us the projected profit potential is approximately $11, or approximately 26 percent.

    Bullish Price Objective is a secondary indicator; however, if the current price is very close to the Bullish Price Objective, it means that much of the potential gain has already been made. Further gains are always possible

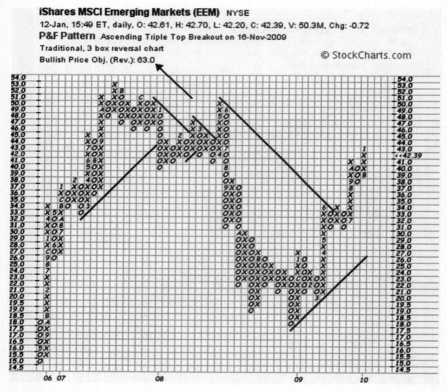

FIGURE 12.3 Bullish Price Objective
Chart courtesy of StockCharts.com

and do occur with regularity, but the farther you are from the Bullish Price Objective when you buy, the larger potential gain you might enjoy.

In this example, EEM has approximately a 26 percent potential gain and so will get 1 point on our matrix.

MACD Histogram Less than 10 Daily Bars Positive: 1 Point

In this section we're going to take a look at MACD Histograms and how to score them.

Figure 12.4 shows us the MACD histogram at the bottom of the chart, the rising and descending blocks. Studying MACD at the bottom of Figure 12.4, let's turn our focus to the histogram highlighted by the arrow and the vertical boxes above and below the zero line that track momentum as we discussed earlier. Here we want to determine and score how long the MACD histogram has been in the current trend. The easiest way

FIGURE 12.4 MACD Histogram
Chart courtesy of StockCharts.com

to do this is to set the chart on a three-month time frame and count the number of bars in the current trend.

In Figure 12.4, the blue bars turned positive in late 2009, and, counting the bars, we find that the trend has been positive for eight bars, or eight trading days, as each bar represents one trading day.

The theory here is simple: When momentum shifts to positive as it does in this example highlighted by the arrow, this could be a good time to enter a trade. Entering a trade soon after a shift in momentum often yields the best results because other traders notice the same pattern and jump on board a newly developing trend. The longer the short-term, daily trend stays in one direction, the more likely it is that it will eventually shift as the trade grows "stale" and that's why you count bars to see where in the trend you are.

Another hint at how the trend is developing is to observe the trend of the bar heights as the days pass. As the trend continues, we can see if it's getting stronger or weaker by observing the height of the bars. Taller bars represent a trend getting stronger while shrinking boxes represent weakening momentum.

For our purposes, if a daily MACD histogram has 10 bars or less, we assign 1 point to the potential trade. We do this because at 10 days or less, there is a good chance that the positive momentum will carry forward for several weeks if confirmed by our other signals. The closer to the crossover point you enter the trade the better, and once a momentum trade gets very long there is greater chance for profit taking and selling pressure to increase and for prices to decline for the short to intermediate term.

So this trade gets 1 point for MACD histogram less than 10 days positive.

RSI Indicator Below 70: 1 point

Our next calculation is Figure 12.5 where we study the RSI. In this figure we see that RSI in the upper grid is at 56.65, well below the 70 that would represent overbought and in fact, is just starting to decline from close to 70, indicating that it is just coming off overbought levels.

If you remember our earlier discussion of RSI, readings above 70 are overbought zones and readings below 30 are oversold zones. The theory here is that if a security is oversold, there is greater profit potential because prices are low and it could be due for a bounce. Conversely, if it's above 70, it's considered overbought and prices are high and so there is potentially less profit potential and greater chance of a pullback.

In general, the old adage "buy low and sell high" is valid and RSI is one method for determining if you're buying on the high or low side of recent price activity.

FIGURE 12.5 RSI below 70
Chart courtesy of StockCharts.com

Looking at Figure 12.5 highlighted by the arrow, the RSI is declining and so you have to make a judgment here whether to wait for it to decline farther or if enough of a pullback has already occurred. This is an example of why one has to study several indicators so we can get confirmation of directional moves rather than relying on just one or two.

For now, RSI is below 70 and so this potential trade gets 1 point for RSI below 70.

Positive Relative Strength to S&P 500: 1 Point

In this section, we are going to check the relative strength of EEM against the S&P 500 and score one point if the relative strength of your potential security is stronger than the underlying benchmark.

In Figure 12.6, we see that EEM: $SPX, or EEM's relative strength to the S&P 500, is above the trend line and in a strong uptrend so we know that

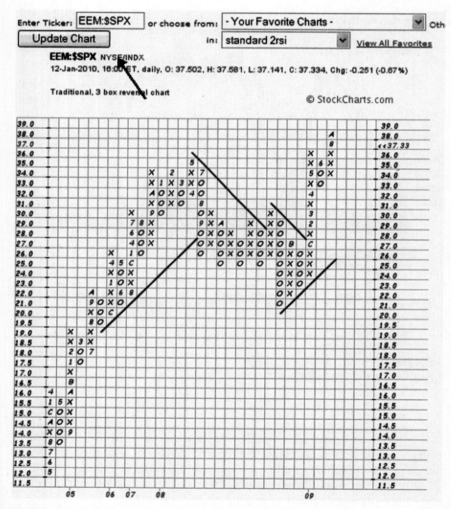

FIGURE 12.6 Relative Strength Compared to S&P 500
Chart courtesy of StockCharts.com

EEM's relative strength is stronger than the S&P 500's. And so we score 1 point for this parameter. So now it's time to add this all up and see what kind of score EEM gets. To do this, you can use the matrix shown in the next section or build one of your own design.

SCORING THE INDICATORS

In Table 12.1, you see this trade is a perfect 6 and would certainly be worth considering taking a position in; however, it's not often that you'll find a perfect 6 and then you must consider the variables of each indicator.

Factors to Consider

The P&F Buy Signal, P&F Trend, and Relative Strength are slower to respond to trend changes and are longer term in nature, while MACD Histogram <10 Bars is shorter term and makes faster changes. P&F Price Objective >10 percent and RSI below 70 are general indicators of where in the trade the security might be.

TABLE 12.1 Scoring Matrix

Security Symbol	P&F Buy Signal	P&F Trend	P&F Price Objective >10 percent	MACD Histogram Matches Weekly and <10 Daily Bars Positive	RSI Below 70	Positive Relative Strength	Total Score
EEM	1	1	1	1	1	1	6

Point and Figure Chart on a Buy Signal: 1 point
Point and Figure Chart Positive Trend: 1 point
Point and Figure Chart Bullish Price Objective >10 percent: 1 point
MACD Daily Histogram Less than 10 Daily Bars Positive and Matches Weekly: 1 Point
RSI below 70: 1 point
Positive Relative Strength: 1 point

Traders and investors with a longer term view will want to rely more heavily on the P&F Buy, Relative Strength, and Trend Indicators while shorter term traders will rely more heavily on the daily MACD indicator and shorter term RSI readings.

So you'll have to do your own scoring and decide which kind of trader you are and where you want to put the most bias. But the bottom line is this: Trades with the highest scores tend to have the most likelihood of success.

Now let's run our analysis on a second trade, DBA, the ProShares Agriculture Trust. Starting with Figure 12.7 we see that DBA is on a buy signal with a Bullish Price Objective and the last column in Xs.

So we're on a buy signal and the current price of $26.27 is about $12 away from the Price Objective of $38, or approximately 46 percent of gain is possible. However, we see that it is below its trend line, the Bearish

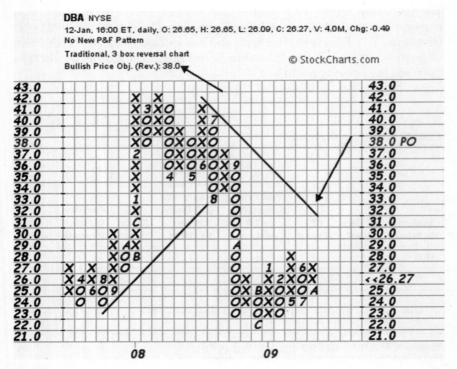

FIGURE 12.7 DBA ProShares Agriculture
Chart Courtesy of StockCharts.com

Resistance Line, highlighted by the descending arrow on the right side of the chart.

Moving on to Figure 12.8, we take a look at RSI. On the RSI portion of Figure 12.8, we see that DBA is below 50 and declining, while the MACD at the bottom of the chart is just about to cross over to the negative and generate a sell signal.

In Figure 12.9 (see p. 126) we see that DBA's Relative Strength is in a column of Os and below the Bearish Resistance Line and so the Relative Strength of DBA is inferior or less than the S&P 500.

Table 12.2 (see p. 126), the Scoring Matrix, shows how DBA scores.

From this exercise, we can conclude that DBA isn't as good a trade as EEM and that EEM has a higher probability of success.

Now let's look at another trade, SLV, iShares Silver Trust in Figure 12.10 (see p. 127). In Figure 12.10 we see that SLV is on a Point and Figure "buy" signal with a Bullish Price Objective of $24.5. Here we see a new

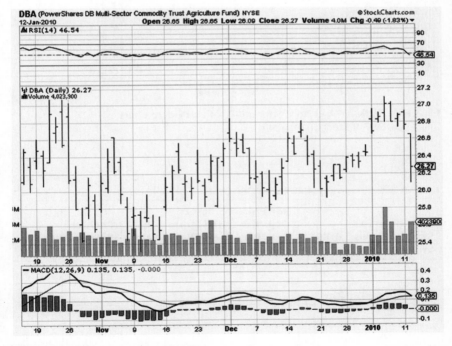

FIGURE 12.8 DBA RSI and MACD
Chart courtesy of StockCharts.com

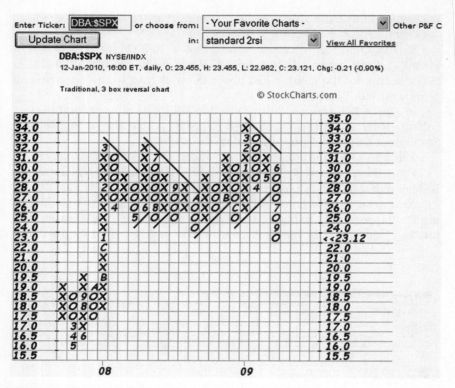

FIGURE 12.9 DBA Relative Strength Point and Figure Chart
Chart courtesy of StockCharts.com

TABLE 12.2 Scoring Matrix with DBA Scores

Security Symbol	P&F Buy Signal	P&F Trend	P&F Price Objective >10 percent	MACD Histogram <10 Bars Positive	RSI Below 70	Positive Relative Strength	Total Score
EEM	1	1	1	1	1	1	6
DBA	1	0	1	0	1	0	3

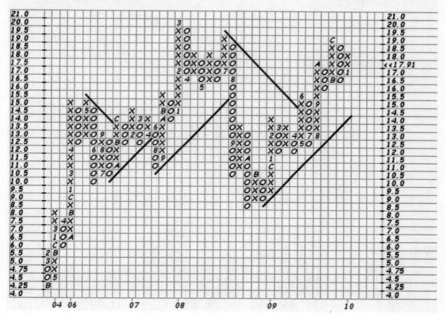

FIGURE 12.10 iShares Silver Trust (SLV)
Chart courtesy of StockCharts.com

element regarding the Price Objective and that is the (rev) which means that it has been revised. With a current price of approximately $18, SLV has a forecast price objective of $6 higher and so a potential project profit of roughly 33 percent. It is above its Bullish Support Line and so in a positive trend.

Moving on to Figure 12.11, we will take a look at the other parameters of SLV. In Figure 12.11, we see that RSI is descending towards 50 and that MACD turned up in early 2010 and has six positive bars on the MACD Histogram.

Moving on to Figure 12.12, we will take a look at Relative Strength on the Point and Figure Chart. Looking at Figure 12.12, SLV: $SPX, we see that SLV is below the Bearish Resistance Line and in a column of zeroes and so its relative strength is weaker than the S&P 500's.

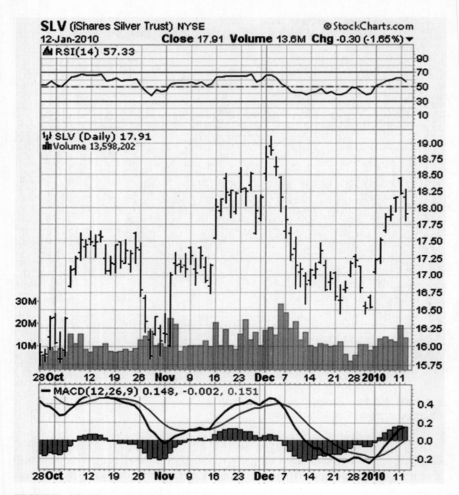

FIGURE 12.11   iShares Silver Trust
Chart courtesy of StockCharts.com

And so SLV would look like this on our matrix in Table 12.3

So we can conclude that EEM and SLV have the highest scores and potentially the highest probability for profit.

At this point, you have to decide which trades you want to take or make a subjective judgment based on other factors like stop-loss points, risk per trade, and your own personal comfort level.

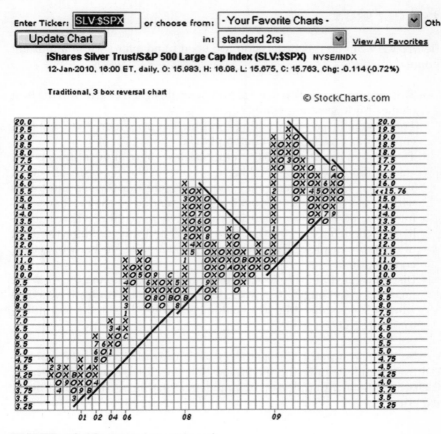

FIGURE 12.12 SLV Relative Strength
Chart courtesy of StockCharts.com

TABLE 12.3 Scoring Matrix with SLV Scores

Security Symbol	P&F Buy Signal	P&F Trend	P&F Price Objective >10 percent	MACD Histogram <10 Bars Positive	RSI Below 70	Positive Relative Strength	Total Score
EEM	1	1	1	1	1	1	6
DBA	1	1	0	0	0	1	3
SLV	1	1	1	1	1	0	5

CONCLUSION

Before we wrap up this discussion, we need to go over several important points:

- This system is based on several principals designed to give you the best chance for a profitable trade.
- This system is based on getting confirmation from more than one indicator for any trade you're contemplating.
- This system is based on discovering trades where momentum has just shifted direction and is picking up steam in the opposite direction. Therefore, trades with recent Point and Figure Buy Signals and trades with recent transitions to positive MACD tend to be the most successful. The trick to this is not getting caught in a "head fake" where it looks like it's changing direction but then doesn't and you get whipsawed out of the trade or pick up a quick loss. And that takes us back to getting confirmation.
- Discipline is vital for following the scoring system no matter what the financial press might be saying. Many of my best trades have come when it seemed like that just couldn't possibly be right, but the indicators were right.

So when you put it all together, you can identify and analyze potential trades and quantify the likelihood that they'll have a positive result, then enter them with a degree of confidence that most traders just never experience.

CHAPTER 13

Getting Out is Harder Than Getting In

M ost amateur traders and investors spend a lot of time contemplating how to get into a position. Technical traders analyze their charts, fundamentalists pour over annual reports and Morningstar reviews, and the really clueless watch financial TV in search of hot tips.

But professionals know that getting in is the easy part. The hard part and, one could argue the most important part of any trade or investment, is knowing when to get out. Professionals will establish their exit plan before they even enter the position so they know when and where they're going to step aside with a profit or with a loss that is predetermined and limited.

In this chapter we're going to look at the important subjects of risk management, exit planning, and specific exit strategies designed to make your trading more reliable and profitable.

SELECTING WHAT YOU WANT TO TRADE: THE OTHER SIDE OF THE COIN

Most people approach their investing or trading analysis by considering how much money they can make on a specific position. What's the potential reward? How big is the profit going to be? And they tend to choose the position with the greatest reward because it's just human nature to want to experience as much pleasure as possible in as short a time as possible.

But professionals approach this whole process from the other side of the coin. How much can they lose in a given trade? How much will the worst possible pain be? And can they stand the pain and take the loss without blowing themselves up?

This dichotomy in approaches is exactly why professionals tend to be successful and amateurs tend to go broke. Whenever you enter a trade, don't think about how much you could make but about how much you could lose.

Risk management always comes first.

Many times you will find awesome trades that you'll have to walk away from because the most reasonable stop-loss points are too far away for prudent amounts of risk and portfolio management.

So there are really two separate but related subjects here. One is the subject of exit strategies and the other is the topic of risk management, different but both equally important for survival and success.

You absolutely must know how and when to exit a trade and you must know how to size your trades and your risk correctly based upon your account size. No matter how much research you do or how hard you try, you will still suffer losing trades, no doubt about it. And so the key is to keep the losses small and appropriate for your account size so that you can weather a bad streak and still stay in the game.

At the end of the day, we all want to make money, but to make money we need money, and we can't lose all our money by risking too much at any one time, by getting greedy or impatient, or by overweighting any one trade because it looks like it's going for the moon.

GETTING OUT OF A TRADE: HOW, WHEN, WHERE

So now you're in a trade and it's going well or maybe not so well.

This is a pretty simple business. When the numbers are green and getting bigger you're happy, or if you're a professional money manager, your clients are happy. And when the numbers are red and getting smaller, you're finding yourself not able to sleep at night, getting an irregular heartbeat, and afraid to turn on your computer in the morning to see how poorly your positions are faring.

In this section we're going to talk about ways to take the stress out of trading when it's not going well and how to make it more fun by taking profits off the table when that opportunity arises.

Stop Losses: What They Are and How to Use Them

Much has been written about stop losses and if they're good or bad, if they hurt or help you, and my view is that it's vital to have some form of stop loss in place, or at least in mind, so that you know how much risk you're taking before you enter a trade.

In my view, trading without stop-loss points is a lot like driving your car without insurance; you have unlimited liability and unlimited risk of loss, at least unlimited down to zero value of your investment.

Stop-loss points and how to use them are probably the most important and least understood aspect of active trading. I say most important because I'll say it again and again: It's just as important, or more important, to know when to exit a trade as it is to know when to enter a trade.

The whole subject of stop losses and risk management can appear to be complicated but it's not as hard or onerous as it first seems. In this section, I'm going to outline several methods for setting stop-loss points so you'll have a menu from which to choose. The discussion will start with money management stops and how to determine them and, then place a money management stop. After that, we'll discuss several types of stop-loss points and how to use them depending on your trading style and time horizons. We'll also talk about risk management as it relates to your overall portfolio because every trade must start with a risk analysis, not a profit analysis, for it to be successful.

As I said earlier, most people buy an ETF or stock or mutual fund thinking about how much they can make without regard for how much they can lose. This system takes exactly the opposite approach, risking the correct amount which then gives you a better shot at being consistently profitable.

And finally, I'll walk you through a step-by-step process for choosing an initial money management stop-loss point, a trailing stop-loss point as the trade moves, and exit strategies depending on what happens during the course of the trade.

Money Management Stop-Loss Points Every trade should start with a money management stop-loss point so that you know how much you're putting at risk from the outset. This is a critical piece of information because you don't ever want to take excessive risk in any one trade.

There are several ways to set a money management stop:

- Fixed percentage
- Volatility based
- Using support levels

I believe that the most effective and successful money management stops employ a combination of all three of these techniques, but everyone is different and some people prefer one or a combination of these.

Fixed Percentage Money Management Stop Loss Points This is very easy to calculate and depends entirely on personal preference. It's a very arbitrary number but is important to consider your personal makeup and risk tolerance in order to be successful.

If you know that you couldn't bear losing more than 5 percent on any one trade, then 5 percent should be your money management stop. If you're okay with 10 percent, then no more than 10 percent should be your number, even when considering all of the other factors involved in setting stop loss points. To calculate a fixed percentage stop, simply take the current price of the security you're interested in and multiply by the appropriate factor which we'll take a closer look at in Figure 13.1.

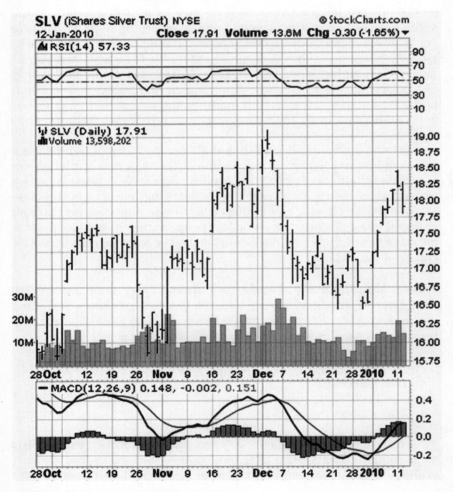

FIGURE 13.1 Money Management Stop
Chart courtesy of StockCharts.com

For instance, if you want a 10 percent stop-loss point and the security is currently trading at $17.91 as in Figure 13.1, you would multiply $17.91 × .90 to get $16.12 for your stop-loss point. The other way to do it would be to multiply $17.91 × .10 and then subtract that number from $17.91. That is: $17.91 × .10 = $1.79. $17.91 − $1.79 = $16.12. So once you do this, you know that your max loss per share of this stock or ETF or mutual fund will be $1.79.

Volatility Based Stop-Loss Points   Volatility based stop-loss points are a more sophisticated way of setting stop-loss points that take into consideration recent volatility of the security. The idea here is to give the security "room to breathe" when you first enter the trade.

The easiest way to set a volatility based stop loss is depicted in Figure 13.2. The four steps include:

1. Go to a chart program like Stockcharts.com or bigcharts.com and pull up the chart you're interested in.
2. Look at the price bars for the last seven trading days.
3. Figure or estimate the average daily range between the highs and lows for the last seven days.
4. Double the amount of the average daily range and this becomes your stop loss.

Looking at Figure 13.2, your calculation would look like this for the last seven days of the SLV chart, starting with the farthest bar on the right and moving to the left for seven bars total. Therefore, your stop loss point would be $.60 less than the last closing price of $17.91, or $17.31.

Day	Low	High	Difference between high and low
No. 1	$17.80	$18.30	$ .50
No. 2	$18.20	$18.45	$ .25
No. 3	$17.90	$18.20	$ .30
No. 4	$17.85	$18.10	$ .25
No. 5	$17.70	$17.90	$ .20
No. 6	$17.20	$17.60	$ .15
No. 7	$17.00	$17.25	$ .25

Sum of the Differences: $2.10
Average Difference: $2.60 ($2.10/7 = .30)
Double the Difference: $ .60

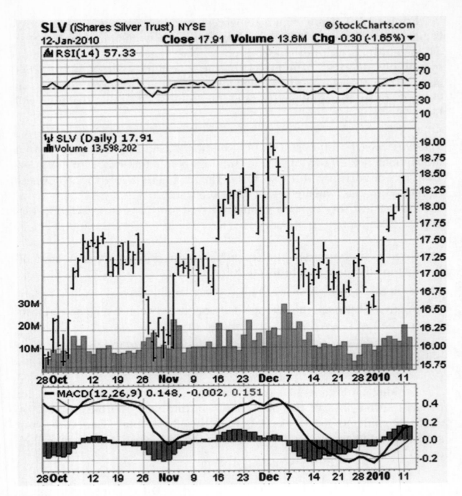

FIGURE 13.2 Volatility-Based Stop Loss
Chart courtesy of StockCharts.com

Comparing that stop-loss point to our percent-based money management stop in the first example, we see that $17.31 is less than our
10 percent money management stop and so we could use either one and
still remain in our comfort zone of losing as much as 10 percent on
this trade.

You can do the actual calculation to figure out the average of the last
seven days but many traders just look at the last seven bars, pick the one

that seems like a medium length, figure out the difference between high and low, and double that figure. This is a time saver and perfectly acceptable.

Setting Stops Based on Support Levels   Probably the most effective way to set stop-loss points is to find significant support levels and set your stop-loss points below that level. Support levels are areas of congestion on the charts to which prices descended, stopped, and then turned around. The theory here is that at significant support levels, buyers reentered the market before and so it's likely they will do so again unless there is a change in trend, in which case, the support levels will be broken.

Moving from right to left in Figure 13.3, we find support levels around $17.80, $17.50, $17.25 and $16.50. These areas are easy to pick out where the bottom of the bars tends to bunch up and form a flat spot.

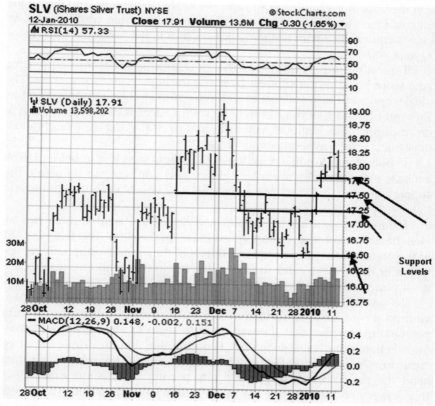

FIGURE 13.3 Support Levels
Chart courtesy of StockCharts.com

Typically, the farther away you set your stop-loss point, the less chance you have of being stopped out but the more risk you will be taking. So, comparing the three points previously discussed, we see the following:

10 percent Stop-Loss Point: $16.12
Volatility Stop-Loss Point: $17.31
Support Based Stop-Loss Point: $17.80, $17.50, $17.25, $16.50

Comparing these three points, you have to decide whether or not to take this trade, and if you're going to, where are you going to set your stop. This is where judgment and experience come into play because setting stop-loss points is part art and part science.

In this example, your best chance of success is most likely placing a stop-loss point somewhere below $16.50 which is below major support, below the volatility stop-loss point, and below the 10 percent stop loss point. So you'll have all three criteria working in your favor, but you'll have to decide if you can live with a slightly greater loss in the event the trade turns against you.

Typically, support levels are the most reliable indicator and placing your stops below major support gives you the best chance for success. The ideal stop-loss point would meet all three criteria but isn't always possible. Two out of three give you a better chance for success than just one, and in order of reliability, support, volatility, and fixed percentage would be the most successful way to plan your stops.

In our example, you'd want to set the actual stop loss at below $16.50 because even numbers are a bad choice and you want to be below the support level at a point that's not obvious, which even numbers tend to be.

Figure 13.4 shows both support and resistance trend lines as well as clear depictions of where support levels are on the chart. You'll notice that in the areas where prices tend to bunch up, they tend to stop moving upwards or downwards, and so just below the lower trend line would be a great place to put a stop loss.

As you're deciding where to place your stops, you must determine your own comfort level for amount of risk per trade. I can tell you from personal experience that the trading gods seem to have a way of knowing when you're overextended or uncomfortable and they drive the price right down to your stop-loss point, take you out of the market, and then send the price soaring upwards again, leaving you behind with a loss that stings and locking you out of the profit you hoped you were going to make.

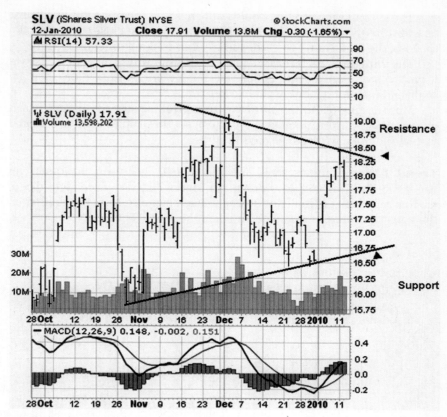

FIGURE 13.4 Support and Resistance Trend Lines
Chart courtesy of StockCharts.com

Trailing Stop-Loss Points What we want to have happen, of course, is to have the trade move in our favor, so let's start with that scenario.

At whatever interval you choose, daily—every other day, or once per week—you need to check the price of the security and look for support levels which may be higher, but not lower than your money management stop, and then set a stop-loss point beneath those levels. The effect of this is that as the price moves upward, your stop will move upwards behind it, first minimizing your risk, then moving to around break-even and then into a profitable position. At some point, the market will turn downwards and hit your stop-loss point and automatically close the position.

The second scenario that could happen is that the price moves against us and stops us out of our position. In this case, we just close the trade, take the loss, the funds move to cash, and we start looking for another trade.

The third scenario is that the price moves sideways and in that case we leave the stop in place and either wait for the price to move or close the trade and look for a more profitable situation.

Most trading platforms allow you to set trailing stop-loss points based on percentage or price points and you can set these up as open orders and just let the trade work as the days progress.

Trend Lines   Traders more interested in longer term positions can use trend lines for stop-loss points. In Figure 13.5, the ascending diagonal line represents a trend line and significant support, so in this depiction, the long- term change would occur when the X or O bar crossed below the

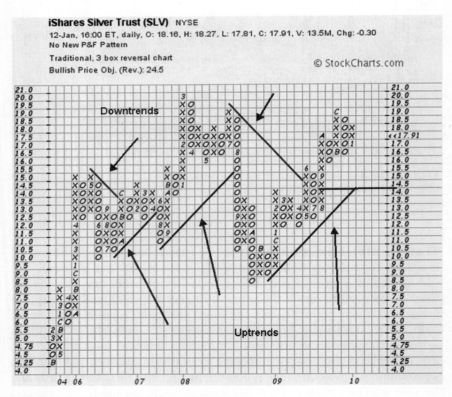

FIGURE 13.5   Point and Figure Trend Lines
Chart courtesy of StockCharts.com

blue line at $65. This is a wide stop of almost $25 from the current price and so losses could be as much as 28 percent. Trend lines are excellent stop-loss points for longer term traders.

In Figure 13.5 we see the Bullish Support Line extending up from a low of approximately $9.00 to approximately $14.25. These lines tend to act as barriers to price action as you can see how the columns of Xs and Os come down to near this line and then continue their rise up and to the right.

In this example, if the columns of Xs and Os were to descend to and break through the Bullish Support Line at approximately $14.50, we could assume that a major trend change had taken place and that the next directional move could be down.

Point and Figure Sell Signals   Another excellent stop-loss point is the Point and Figure Sell Signal depicted in Figure 13.6 by the last column

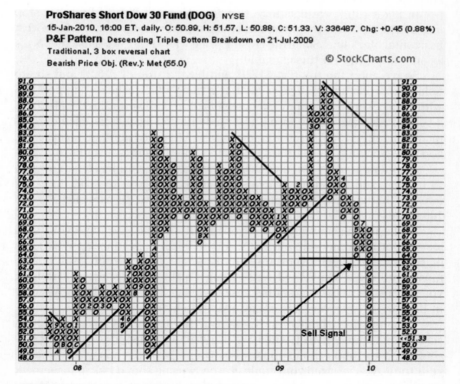

FIGURE 13.6   Point and Figure Sell Signal
Chart courtesy of StockCharts.com

of Os and the P&F Pattern which says, "Descending Triple Bottom Break-down." Highlighted in Figure 13.6 by the horizontal line and arrow, we see where the last descending column of Os broke a double bottom at about $64 and when we look at the caption we see that this was a Descending Triple Bottom Breakdown on July 21, 2009.

When a Point and Figure Chart goes to a sell signal there's a high possibility of prices moving lower or at least sideways for the near term. Therefore, this could be an excellent place to exit the trade and take profits or losses that may exist. In Figure 13.6 we see that prices continued to drop and now stand at $51.33, so getting out back when prices were at $64 would have helped sidestep substantial losses.

Placing and Using Stop Losses   I just can't emphasize how important stop losses are to your trading success. And because of that, in my opinion the best way to set up a stop loss is to do it immediately after you open the trade. This is probably the most critical element to your trading success. The mechanics of this are simple.

In Figure 13.7, we decide to buy 100 shares of SLV and place a stop loss at $16.25, below the lowest level of support as indicated by the lowest horizontal black line. Since the closing price was $17.91, we'll use that price as our entry price for this example.

So we enter the trade at $17.91 and have a stop of $16.25 and so are risking approximately 9.0 percent on this trade which is below support and within the 10 percent money management stop that we earlier decided was a comfortable amount to lose if this trade turned against us. So, now, immediately after you open the trade, you would place another open order, good 'til cancelled, to sell 100 shares of SLV at the stop price of $16.25.

All online trading companies like Schwab, Ameritrade, etc., allow you to do this, and if you use a live stock broker, all you have to do is tell him/her that you want to place an open order, good 'til cancelled, to sell 100 shares of SLV at the stop price of $16.25.

That's it, and now you have your trade on and you have your stop loss—your insurance—in place. Of course, if there is a market meltdown or some catastrophic event, the stop loss might not protect you, but on most days it will. The only defense against a catastrophic event is to limit your exposure to the market because on a day like 9/11 or Black Monday in 1987, there were very few, if any, places to hide.

The only way to limit your exposure in this instance is through position size and risk management, which we'll talk about in just a moment. But barring a disaster, at this point you've used your signals to choose and confirm your trade, you've sized your trade correctly using sound risk management principles, and you've determined and placed your stop-loss point. Now, there's nothing else to do except watch and see how the trade develops.

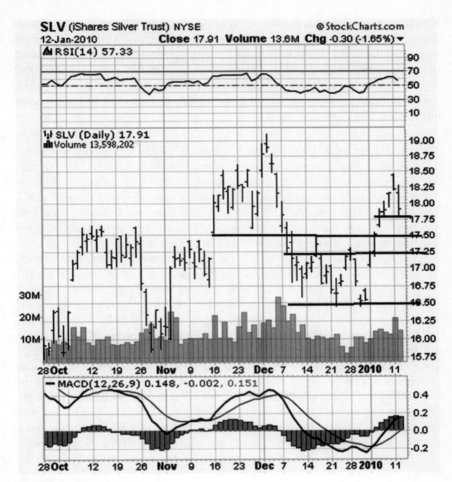

FIGURE 13.7 Setting a Stop Loss
Chart courtesy of StockCharts.com

Special Note for Mutual Fund Investors Regarding Stop Losses

Your mutual fund will not allow you to preset a stop-loss point but you can follow the exact same methodology outlined above and then determine a "mental stop-loss point." Write this number down, and when the NAV of your mutual fund closes below this level, enter a "sell" order for the next day. This way you'll exit your position at the earliest possible moment after your stop loss is hit.

Mutual funds don't have the flexibility of ETFs or individual stocks when it comes to order entry or exit; however, everything we're discussing in this book is perfectly compatible with mutual fund trading.

Final Notes on Stop Losses   We've spent a lot of time on stop losses and how to use them and for very good reason. Exiting a trade correctly is probably the single most important and most difficult skill to master and, in my opinion, the single major reason that traders fail.

So here are a couple of things to keep in mind about stop-loss points and risk management that will help you find more success in your trading endeavors:

- *Always, always use a stop loss point and preset it as an open order if you can.* This removes the temptation to readjust it as the price of your security moves toward it and threatens to take you out of the position. The only time you might want to consider not doing this is when you're working with leveraged ETFs due to their inherent volatility on a daily basis, which could lead to whipsaws. We'll discuss leveraged ETFs and how to trade them in greater detail in a later chapter.
- *Once you enter a trade and set a stop loss, walk away.* Don't tinker with it. Don't try to outguess the market. If the trade moves in your favor, move up your trailing stop, and at some point, the market will reverse and take you automatically out of the trade. It's extremely difficult to get out by taking profits and then getting in later on dips and trying to catch every little up and down of the market. Overtrading is the hallmark of the amateur.
- *Readjust the way you think about gains and losses.* The amateur considers a gain as profit even when it's an unrealized gain but doesn't consider a losing position a loss until he sells the position. This is the exact opposite of how a successful trader thinks. The pro knows that a gain isn't a gain until you close the trade and a loss is a loss as soon as the numbers turn red. Therefore, a professional trader will strictly limit losses to small amounts of equity and close the trade when it hits that predetermined level while the amateur will "hang on just awhile, it will come back."
- *A loss is not a loss unless you let it get out of control.* Small losses are a normal part of active trading and must be accepted in order to be successful. A loss is simply exiting a position that didn't work out and moving on to the next opportunity, nothing more. And if you set your risk correctly, it shouldn't hurt you in the long run at all.

RISK MANAGEMENT AND POSITION SIZE

I mentioned at the outset of this chapter that Risk Management is one of the cornerstones of successful trading. I'm constantly surprised that so few investors know about this concept or how to apply it to protect themselves from catastrophic losses.

There are two elements to this subject: how to control risk and how to appropriately size your position based on risk in a particular trade and the size of your trading account.

Returning to our previous example of SLV and our stop loss of 9.0 percent, we've decided that we're going to buy SLV at $17.91/share with a stop loss point of $16.25. The next question that's equally important to our stop-loss position is how many shares to buy. And again, this number must be based on how much we can afford to lose, not how much we hope to gain.

Determining Position Size

Now that we know what percentage of our investment we are going to risk on a specific trade, we have to decide how many dollars we're going to risk, or put another way, how many shares are we going to buy? What is our position size going to be? Making a correct decision here is critical to your long-term success as a trader or investor.

Generally speaking, the common rule of thumb is that traders shouldn't risk more than 2 to 3 percent of total equity on any one trade, and certainly no more than 5 percent. Many professionals suggest that risk per trade should only be 1 percent of your total portfolio but the amount you settle on is your own personal preference. The key thing here is not taking too much risk per trade because the idea is for you to be able to survive trades that move against you and stay in the game no matter what happens.

For our purposes, we'll use 3 percent as our number for determining position size. This means that you could have more than 30 losing trades in a row before you went broke. And that's the whole purpose of limiting risk in each position. Because you will have losses; that's just part of active trading, and that's why limiting risk in each position is paramount for success so that the losses don't hurt you in the long run.

To complete our example, let's say we're trading with a $50,000 account, so 3 percent of $50,000 is $1,500 which is the maximum amount we want to risk on a single trade. Since we know that we're going to risk 9 percent on this trade, we have to figure out what the total dollar amount of the trade should be. To do this, we divide $1,500 by 9 percent which gives us $16,666 as the maximum position size of this account ($1,500/.09 = $16,666).

We're going to buy SLV at a limit price of $17.91 so the maximum number of shares we should buy is 930 ($16,666/$17.91 = 930). Now we know that we're going to buy 930 shares for $17.91. If the price declines to $16.25 and we get stopped out, we'll lose $1.66/share or a total of $1,543.00 ($1.66 × 930 = $1,543). And $1,543 is 3 percent of our $50,000 trading account, so if this trade goes against us we won't be wiped out and we'll have plenty of other opportunities to make money on other trades.

As I write this, the markets have been experiencing volatility levels unseen since the 1930s. Highly volatile markets are also highly risky markets and so a very strong argument could be made for taking smaller than normal position sizes during periods of high market volatility like the environment we currently face.

Position sizing is all important to your success as an active trader and any expert will tell you it's better to take smaller risks and make smaller gains per trade and live to fight another day when the market moves against you.

EXITING A TRADE OR "WHAT NOW?"

Now that we're in our trade, we have our stop set, and we're watching. At this point, only one of three things can happen:

1. The trade could move against us and we'll get stopped out at our money management stop-loss point.
2. The trade could move in our favor and the price could continue climbing.
3. The trade could move sideways and not stop us out or move upwards and then weaken.

Scenario No. 1: A Quick Loss but Easy to Manage

In Scenario No. 1, the trade moves against us and we get stopped out. If we get stopped out, our funds move to cash and we look for the next trade. The key thing here is not to intervene with the trade or reset our stops in hopes of "saving" the trade.

Scenario No. 2: The Trade Does What We Want and We Feel Good

Scenario No. 2 is what we're looking for, and if the trade moves in our favor, that is, starts climbing, we move the stop-loss point up with it based on the support levels we discussed earlier or we have set a trailing stop-loss point that automatically follows the price as it moves upward.

The effect of this trailing stop is that first we'll start limiting our loss from the bigger initial number and as the trade moves, the stop will move up day after day, week after week, and as it moves, our risk decreases, then moves to around break-even and finally the stop-loss point is above the point we bought in and so now we have a profit. And we just let our winner run until eventually, the market will reverse and our stop will be hit and the trade will be over.

Scenario No. 3: The Nail Biter

Scenario No. 3 is the most difficult to deal with because we don't know if the position is temporarily stalled and will resume its uptrend or not. In this case, we can maintain our original stop and just wait to see what happens and wait for our stop to take us out or we can close the trade if conditions change and we see signs of weakness in the trade. Sideways markets are universally hated by traders because we want to make money and unless you're extremely skilled at day trading, sideways markets are difficult environments in which to win and oftentimes wind up whipsawing us for loss after loss if volatility is high.

SIGNS OF WEAKNESS

When faced with a sideways market, we can look for other clues to tell us whether to get out or to hang in with the trade and see what happens, even if it means risking our capital in what could be an unfriendly and even hostile environment.

The best set of clues I know of are signs of weakness that can tip us off to the fact that the markets are weakening and that perhaps our trade is going sour. This is a judgment call and one that you will get better at making with experience, but here are three signs of weakness that could cause you to close a trade without waiting for your stop loss to be hit.

RSI

The RSI indicates an overbought condition and the line turns and starts heading downwards. In Figure 13.8, in the top display we see that in recent days, RSI has been near 70 and has now declined to 56.55 and is still pointing downwards, as depicted by the two arrows on the right hand side of the chart.

In Figure 13.8, if we go back to November, we can see another occasion where RSI was near 70 and then started to decline, and that this decline preceded a sharp drop in prices from approximately $110 to a low of just above $102. A turn south by RSI from overbought levels is typically a warning that prices will weaken and so this could be a time when we

FIGURE 13.8 Declining RSI
Chart courtesy of StockCharts.com

might decide to step aside or take some risk off the table by reducing our position size.

MACD Flattens Out

The second sign of weakness is when the MACD lines turn and head towards the zero line. You don't have to wait for the line to cross zero or the histogram to turn negative, because, oftentimes, but not always, when the blue histogram blocks start shrinking, it's a precursor to an impending crossover and drop below the zero line, as seen in Figure 13.9.

In Figure 13.9, MACD is declining, the boxes are shrinking, and while still on a buy signal, price momentum has clearly leveled off. In this instance you can exit the trade early in which case you might risk it turning back upwards or you can wait for MACD to trigger a sell signal when it crosses over the moving average and the histogram turns negative.

Remember that daily MACD is a short-term indicator and so exiting on a daily MACD sell could protect profits or limit losses while you wait for the market to regain its strength and resume its upwards trend.

FIGURE 13.9 Declining MACD
Chart courtesy of StockCharts.com

Point and Figure Sell Signal

The third time to consider exiting a trade ahead of getting stopped out can be seen on the Point and Figure Chart when it goes to a sell signal before your stop loss is hit.

In this case, even though you're still in the trade as far as your stop loss is concerned, one of the primary reasons for entering the trade, a Point and Figure buy signal, no longer exists and typically this would indicate lower prices ahead. This is one of those times when you can say that the trade didn't materialize as planned and the best strategy is to step aside and look for a stronger trade with better upside potential.

Figure 13.10 shows a Point and Figure Sell Signal that could be a great reason to exit this trade. This is a personal preference based on experience and you may miss out on a huge upside move if the P&F pattern reverses to a bullish pattern, which can happen. But if a sell signal is generated, the chart has weakened and prices could be going lower.

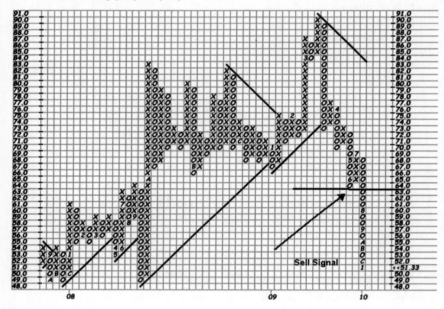

ProShares Short Dow 30 Fund (DOG) NYSE
15-Jan-2010, 16:00 ET, daily, O: 50.89, H: 51.57, L: 50.88, C: 51.33, V: 336487, Chg: +0.45 (0.88%)
P&F Pattern Descending Triple Bottom Breakdown on 21-Jul-2009
Traditional, 3 box reversal chart
Bearish Price Obj. (Rev.): Met (55.0)

FIGURE 13.10   Point and Figure Sell Signal
Chart courtesy of StockCharts.com

Again, just like when you're considering entering a trade, you should
look for confirmation from the other indicators that the trend is actually
changing. This might seem confusing now but as you gain more experience,
you'll get a feel for the strength of a stock and the velocity of the move and
know what you want to do. The worst that can happen is that you'll take
profits too early and miss a further upside move, but that's OK because
there's always another opportunity coming along.

CONCLUSION

In this section we've discussed some of the most important elements of
successful trading: how to set and use stop losses, risk management, and
proper position sizing.

The important thing about stop-loss points is to select a method that feels comfortable and then stick to it with an iron clad discipline. And the most important element of risk management is to properly size your positions so that you have an appropriate amount of risk so that if and when the trade goes against you, the loss will be acceptable and not damage your future potential for success. Far more important than selecting what to trade or how to enter a trade, proper exit techniques will ultimately determine your success or failure.

If you can master these elements of trading, you will be miles ahead of your competition and well on your way to a successful experience as a trader or short-term investor.

CHAPTER 14

The Psychology of Trading

M ost traders and investors assume that the "enemy" is the market or the other investors, traders, and speculators against whom you're competing every day. And this is partially true because as the old saying goes, "the markets are designed to inflict the maximum pain possible upon the maximum number of people possible."

But there is a more subtle and deadly enemy.

THE BIGGEST SINGLE RISK TO YOUR TRADING AND INVESTING SUCCESS IS YOU

That face you see in the mirror is the biggest obstacle to your success. Actually, it's the brain behind the face that's your biggest danger, specifically your ego and emotions.

I don't know of a single trader or investor who hasn't let his or her emotions and ego interfere with their trading and if they're at all truthful, they'll tell you that the biggest losses, the worst mistakes they ever made, were when they didn't follow their system and let their ego and emotions get in the way of their trading discipline. I have learned this the hard way, as have most others who have been trading for any length of time, and I'm here to tell you that it's both painful and expensive.

There's nothing quite as painful as seeing trades go against you and then having the losses compounded by your own errors. There's no greater

pain than entering a prolonged drawdown and wondering if your system is
ever going to work again, or if you're ever going to get back to break even.

As a very successful professional money manager and friend of mine
likes to say, "The only thing more stressful than losing money in the stock
market is losing a lot of money in the stock market." He's right and that's
why we're going to spend some time on the psychology of trading and fully
understand why this element is so critical to your success. We'll look at
some tips, tricks, and techniques to give you an edge and I hope that you'll
be able to sidestep the bad experience of you sabotaging your own success.

BEGIN AT THE BEGINNING

The first step to conquering the psychological aspects of trading or active
money management is to choose a trading style that fits your psychological
makeup. You must trade with a style and system that is comfortable for
you, you must be able to sleep at night and, most importantly, you must
be able to sustain your trading activities over extended periods, some of
which might be extremely painful when the market is moving against you
and your system just doesn't seem to work.

A day trader is a completely different animal from someone who is
comfortable with longer-term positions or the person who just wants to
stay in the market and step aside during the major downturns. You must
decide what kind of trader you are and the only way to do that is to try
out the different styles. Start paper trading an account and try it as a day
trader. Then try it using longer term positions and see what feels better. I
can't tell you how important this is.

You must correctly match your trading style with your personality type
or you are doomed to failure. In the following section, we'll discuss trading
psychology and examine "3 Secrets of Trading Success" that will help you
understand your "humanness" and help get your emotions working for you
instead of against you. We'll also talk about "Trading is War" and "The Zen
of Trading" and which approach might be right for you.

GREED, FEAR, AND THE HERD

Everyone has heard about greed and fear being the two primary driving
forces behind investor decisions. And that is true, because while much
has been written about markets being rational and investors making rational decisions based on earnings reports, price earnings ratios, or technical analysis, my opinion is that markets are not rational, as witnessed

throughout history during times of spectacular bubbles and equally spectacular crashes.

Whenever you see a bubble or a bust, you know greed and fear are at work and irrationality is controlling the markets and this has been seen time and again throughout history.

The Dutch had their tulips, Sir Isaac Newton was wiped out in the South Sea Trading Company's meltdown in 1720, and we've had our own Black Monday in 1987 and the dot.com boom and bust just a few short years ago. Not to mention The Great Recession and Bear Market of 2007–2008.

Greed is simple to understand. People want to make money. But fear is a little more complex in that there are really two types of fear: fear of loss, which we all understand, but also, fear of being left behind.

I believe a key to investment success is learning to control both your greed and your fear, and the solutions are the same for both.

Investors Who Conquer their Emotions

- *Don't overtrade.* In the search for better results or to limit loss, investors tend to overtrade and wind up paying too much in commissions or getting whipsawed by short-term gyrations of the market.
- *Don't take too much risk.* Greed causes investors to take too much risk, either through options, leverage, investing in risky companies, or by taking positions that are too large to be comfortable.
- *Don't go back and look at trades they have sold to see how they "would've done."* When a trade is over, it's over. They don't do post-mortems to see if they were "right" or "wrong" about the market.
- *Don't sell their winners too soon,* unlike most investors who do this and miss out on further gains.
- *Don't hang on to their losers too long.* Most investors find it's hard to admit they were "wrong" and so lose more than they should or could. Ego plays a big role here. People want to be right, but "hang on, it'll come back" is not an investment strategy. Just ask anyone who still owns some of the darlings of the dot.com boom and bust.
- *Don't do daily mental accounting of how they're doing.* They see their whole portfolio, not just the rise and fall of individual positions, and they don't keep a score card of their gains/losses.
- *Don't listen to or believe what you read in the financial media,* who are masters of feeding the herd mentality that successful investors avoid.
- *Take the long view.* They don't talk about their stock picks, winners/losers with friends. They don't follow hot tips. They keep their own counsel. They don't check their holdings online every five minutes.

- *Don't put their egos into their trading.* Pride in a good trade is as harmful as shame or anger or grief over a bad trade. Some trades will go well. Some trades won't go well. It has nothing to do with the investor's intellect or self-worth.
- *Find a good plan and stick with it.* A great batter in baseball only succeeds four out of ten times at the plate. Investing is a marathon, not a sprint.

Most retail investors lose money in the markets because they let fear and greed—their emotions—interfere with their trading success. But the average investor generally can't do this and so average retail investors' returns range from −2.2 percent to +3 percent per year, depending on which study you quote.

Why the poor results? Because average investors can't control their emotions and let fear and greed and ego dominate their trading decisions. While there can never be any guarantee of success, most investors find that understanding fear, greed, and the herd mentality—then learning to manage their emotions—can lead to better outcomes for their investing activity.

THREE SECRETS TO TRADING SUCCESS

You can boil this whole topic down to one element and that is:

Discipline is the key element to success.

It's an element you must develop if you want to be successful. You must be able to methodically stick to your system, day in and day out, and follow your rules and do it repeatedly if you want to be successful.

So, that's all well and good, you might be saying about now, but *how do I do it?*

And it's really pretty simple but incredibly difficult at the same time. Even with years of experience, you'll find that you are battling yourself and working to control your emotions so they don't get in the way of your investment and trading success. I know this from my own experience and it's absolutely the number one reason that people fail at this business—they simply don't have the discipline to be consistent and follow a firm set of rules no matter what happens.

As a side note, this one factor has led to the surge in "black box" or computer-based programs because professionals have recognized the danger of human emotions in trading and have tried to eliminate it from their quantitative systems. This is a nice idea, but in my opinion, it also, falls short of ultimate success, because in the end, the market's action is the sum of human emotion.

Regarding "black box" systems, they have become all the rage with "quants" running Wall Street with their super computers and algorithms, but I agree with Warren Buffett who once said, "Beware of geeks bearing formulas."[1]

Markets Aren't Rational

If they were, we wouldn't have bubbles and crashes. We wouldn't have parabolic rises that outstrip fundamentals nor would we have crashes that don't take fundamentals into account.

So the mechanical programs that try to eliminate human emotion usually work for awhile and then stop as markets change and evolve, much the same way that people do. In fact, there's a well-known saying in the money management business that these systems "work until they don't."

And that's all too true. I've decided that, at least for myself, I'm going to take a mix of the technical trading devices which we've discussed and combine it with some fundamental analysis and sentiment considerations to develop a program that has a good chance of succeeding in any market environment.

But there is simply no question about the fact that you are your greatest enemy and that your emotions will most likely be the cause of your eventual failure if you don't learn how to control and discipline yourself to trade like a professional.

Following are three secrets you can use to help take the emotion out of trading.

Secret No. 1: Follow your Indicators No Matter What!

In this book we've talked about five signals to use to enter a trade and how to score a potential trade. And when you go through that process and find a trade that meets all of our criteria, you should take the trade, no matter how tough it is, no matter how your gut might be telling you something different, or how scary it might be.

I can't tell you how many times my signals have said buy when everything, and I mean everything, I saw on TV or read in the news was telling me to sell. Conversely, I've gotten many sell signals that just couldn't possibly have been right because the market was on such a tear and I was printing money, big money, on a daily basis.

But you know what? You have to follow your indicators. It's just that simple, and when you do, you'll be surprised more often than not by the positive outcomes and the profits.

When your signals say "buy," my opinion is that you should buy and when they say sell, my opinion is that you should sell. It's just that simple but you'll find that it's also sometimes the hardest thing you've ever done.

Secret No. 2: Honor Your Stops

We spent a long time discussing stop-loss points and how to use them, so you already know how important this aspect of active trading really is. But it needs to be said again because so many people go wrong right here.

You must honor your stop-loss points no matter what. Don't change them. Don't do a "mental stop" where you tell yourself you'll just "watch it" and when it goes below your stop-loss point you'll get out. Because you won't. Don't ever tell yourself, "I'll just hang on, it'll come back," because you could be heading for really, really big trouble.

Just think back to the Tech Wreck of 2000 if you need to remind yourself of the disaster that befell so many investors. All of the major markets plunged, and as of 2008 investors who didn't get out are still hanging on and waiting for it to come back. They're still underwater and have lost nearly a decade of their investing lives.

If they had just used a simple trailing stop, they would have walked away with huge gains safely locked in and perhaps their futures would have been changed forever. But what happened instead is that they rode these down into the dirt and were literally wiped out.

I did it to myself during the Tech Wreck or 2000–2002, and maybe you did, too. And I will never do it again. The same thing happened during The Great Recession and Bear Market of 2007–2008. The average guy rode the market down to the "March Lows" that were reached in March 2009, and then got out just before the next uptrend began.

But with a disciplined trading plan, even just a simple major trend following system like "The Simple System" or "Almost As Good As Buy and Hold," they could have avoided this calamity.

Secret No. 3: Place Your Trade and Walk Away

This is the most difficult element we'll discuss in the psychology of trading but perhaps the most important—if you can master this technique, you have a real shot at becoming a highly successful trader.

How many people do you know, including me and maybe you, who are glued to financial television or to their computer screens or are constantly checking stock quotes on their Blackberries or iPhones? This is one of the most deadly habits you can develop and it's one of the toughest habits to break. You'll never completely break it, but if you can take the following steps you'll be a huge leg up on your competition:

- Set your trades up on the weekend or in the evening when the markets are closed and you're not in the heat of battle.
- When your trades are filled, place your stop-loss points as good 'til cancelled open orders for each position you entered.
- Turn off your computer and walk away. And don't check your trading account ever until after the close the next Friday afternoon (much easier said than done, but a good goal nevertheless).
- Now let me tell you, these three steps are difficult, if not impossible to achieve, but you absolutely must accomplish No. 1 and No. 2 to give yourself the best chances for success.

The real challenge is No. 3—turning off your computer and walking away. I've never been able to completely do that but I can tell you that the less time you spend staring at your computer, the fewer times you check your profits/losses, and the less you check your account balance, the more successful you'll be.

And the reasons for this are simple. Money is a very emotional topic.

The very best traders oftentimes don't trade with their own money, which allows them to remain emotionally distant from their trading activities. For those of us who do trade our own money, if you can somehow not think of it as money, but rather as numbers, statistics, or a game, you'll be miles ahead of your competition and have the chance for many more positive outcomes.

Another tip is to not worry or even think about how much you make or lose on a trade, or to judge its success or failure based on a dollar amount. Instead take a technical view of each trade and judge its merits on how closely you followed your system, on the skill and techniques you deployed, and what factors ultimately led to its success or failure. Measuring the outcome in this fashion tends to remove emotion from your trading, and removing emotion removes bad judgment.

Removing emotion and removing bad judgment are the main reasons it's so important to not be constantly checking your computer. If you're constantly checking the action you're bound to get stressed out and let your emotions get in the way if things are going badly. You're bound to be tempted to change your stop or enter a trade you see developing without researching it under the cool, calm conditions of a time when the market is closed. Conversely, when things are going well, it's an emotional high and you'll be beating your chest and proclaiming what a genius you are and all you're really doing here is putting yourself on an emotional roller coaster ride that very likely will end in a painful and expensive crash.

On my web site I say, "Investment success is not a sprint but a marathon," and to survive the rigors of this marathon, a big-picture, detached attitude is key to survival and success. If you can limit your exposure to the heat of the market, lots of good things will happen.

- You'll have more time to be with your family and friends.
- You'll be more successful in your trading.
- You'll sleep better at night and not find yourself being whipsawed by the emotions of the market or the talking heads on television that are being paid to scare the hell out of you.

TRADING AND THE ART OF WAR

Many books have been written about how trading is war and you're in competition with thousands of others around the world in a zero-sum game that is designed to have winners and losers. If this is your view, the competition is formidable to say the least.

You're up against high-speed, high-powered computers that can make split-second decisions based on news before you've even heard it.

You're up against seasoned professionals at big trading desks who can literally move billions around the world at virtually the speed of light.

You're competing with literally millions of people just like yourself, each with a different system or approach that easily could be better and more effective than yours.

So the playing field is rather intimidating, or is it?

Actually, I believe that you have just as good a chance to succeed as anyone else out there. Just look at all the hedge funds that blew up during the great Bear Market of 2007–2008. Look at all the "professional advisors" who lost their clients, as much or more as individuals managed to lose on their own. But if you see trading as "war," then some proven principles for fighting a war might be worth considering.

One of the most famous and effective books on war is *The Art of War* by Sun Tzu. In this classic work, Sun Tzu said that war was a "matter of life and death, a road either to safety or to ruin." I would argue that trading a portfolio is also a matter of life or death or at least seriously important when it comes to your retirement, overall net worth, and financial well being. And it certainly is a road to either safety or ruin.

Sun Tzu goes on to say, "Now the general who wins a battle makes many calculations in his temple ere the battle is fought. The general who loses a battle makes but few calculations beforehand. Thus do many calculations lead to victory and few calculations to defeat: how much more no calculation at all! It is by attention to this point that I can foresee who is likely to win or lose."

Read the previous paragraph above over and over again until you get it. You must prepare well beforehand for battle and many calculations lead to victory and few calculations to defeat. The outcome is certain failure for the unprepared.

I know people who trade on hunches, who trade without a plan and who "wing it," and I'm sure you do, too. And inevitably, they will be losers as Sun Tzu has forecast.

THE FIVE ESSENTIALS FOR VICTORY

I would argue that all of the following points made by Sun Tzu are key elements of success in trading today's complex and fast-moving markets:

1. He will win who knows when to fight and when not to fight.
2. He will win who knows how to handle both superior and inferior forces.
3. He will win whose army is animated by the same spirit throughout all its ranks.
4. He will win who, prepared himself, waits to take the enemy unprepared.
5. He will win who has military capacity and is not interfered with by the sovereign.

Knowing when to take a trade is as important as knowing when not to. Knowing when to exit is critically important, as we've already discussed; you must know when to fight and when not to fight.

Knowing how to handle both superior and inferior forces is vital. Every day you're up against an armada of smart, talented, and well-financed professional traders who are just itching to take your money away from you. This is even truer in the aftermath of the bear market created by The Great Recession, when volumes have plummeted and computer-driven programs and algorithms prowl Wall Street and move markets like they never have before.

As we've already discussed, preparation is vital and a basic requirement for the success of your "army"—your trading discipline must be unified and fully understood and animated by a winning spirit in every dimension of its existence.

And Sun Tzu summarizes by saying, "If you know the enemy and know yourself, you need not fear the result of a hundred battles. If you know yourself but not the enemy, for every victory gained you will also suffer a defeat. If you know neither the enemy nor yourself, you will succumb in every battle."[2]

TRADING WITH THE BUDDHA

I am a mainstream, Western guy, but there is a lot of wisdom to be found in Eastern teachings, particularly as it relates to trading.

Trading is an extremely stressful activity and you'll find that to participate in today's fast moving markets on a long-term basis and survive, you are going to need some very practical survival skills. Among these is the deployment of some sort of relaxation technique. I know traders who meditate, traders who use deep breathing techniques, visualization, or guided imagery. Whatever you decide upon, make it a regular part of your routine and you'll do better and last longer in this high pressured game.

You also need to exercise. This sounds crazy but if you can get away from your computer and get outside and exercise, you'll find yourself feeling stronger and will be more successful in your trading. Some of the best traders I know are absolute physical fitness freaks and gym rats, others are dedicated practitioners of yoga, and more than a few are marathoners and triathletes who do battle with the bulls and bears everyday on Wall Street.

And finally, the correct outlook is important, I would say crucial, to your trading success. We've talked about how some traders approach trading as war, but the inverse approach is to approach trading in a unified and "oneness" with the markets.

I know this sounds like it's out of left field but traders who look at the market as their friend, who approach it as a place where they can go to receive a steady supply of money, fare better over the long term than those who find it to be a hostile and scary place. The old saying, "attitude is everything," certainly applies to the business of being a professional trader.

Looking at Buddhist philosophy, we find "The Noble Eightfold Path." Let's take a look at Buddha's eight points for enlightened living:

1. *Right View:* Right view refers to how you look at things, your perspective and understanding. Is the market your enemy? Are you afraid of it or do you embrace its challenges as an opportunity?

2. *Right Thinking:* Is your thinking focused on screwing the other guy or destroying your opponent so you can be successful or do you just

want to come to the market and make money, knowing that you're not hurting anyone in the process? And you can do this with ETFs and stocks because, unlike commodities, it is not a zero-sum game.

3. *Right Mindfulness:* This is right attention and awareness, just keeping your mind and your focus on the ball. Don't listen to the financial press. Don't listen to "hot tips" or others' opinions because nobody knows any more than you do. If you lose your focus and drift from your system, you are doomed to fail.

4. *Right Speech:* Do you compare notes with other traders, friends? If you do, stop. How many times have you said, "What do you think the market's going to do?" or "Are you bullish or bearish?" This type of talk can only hurt your potential for trading success. The message here is to keep your own counsel. Don't listen to others' opinions or express your own. The closer you can get to working in a vacuum, the better.

5. *Right Action:* This is as simple as "just do the right thing." Approach trading as an ethical and honest activity and the laws of "karma" will reward you. Develop the right system for you and use it religiously.

6. *Right Diligence:* This just means being diligent and doing the right thing every day, over and over again. Follow your system. Be disciplined. Don't vary from your methods.

7. *Right Concentration:* Focus on your system and your trading methodology and nothing else. The only time you will really hurt yourself is if you lose your concentration and let all of the "noise" sway your trading decisions or make you take your eye off the ball.

8. *Right Livelihood:* Is trading the right livelihood for you? If not, you'll have to decide what you might want to do instead. Make sure that you find the method that suits you best, as we discussed earlier, and you'll be both happy and successful.[3]

WHAT HAPPENS WHEN YOUR SYSTEM STOPS WORKING

There's a well-known phrase among active managers and traders that goes like this, "it works until it doesn't." This old saying is exactly correct because at some point in your trading career, your system will stop working. There are many possible reasons for this.

The most likely cause is you. You've changed something. You fade your system. You're not paying attention to your signals. You're doing something subtly different than you were before.

If you start taking consistent losses, the first thing to do is look in the mirror and go back over your trading journal and see if you're the cause of your problems. Ninety percent of the time you will be the cause and that's an easy fix. Just stop trading for awhile, and then go back to paper trading and then start trading small amounts and slowly scale back in as you rediscover your discipline, self-confidence, and equilibrium.

If the problem isn't you, then you need to look at your system. If it was working before and isn't now, then something external has changed.

The markets are a constantly changing, evolving, and dynamic organism, the sum total of millions, even billions of individual trading decisions, perceptions, and actions. If the market has somehow materially changed, and it will, your system might have to change with it. If volatility is high and you're getting whipsawed, you will have to find a way to cope with that. If your system no longer picks up trend changes or if there is no trend, you'll have to cope with that.

Usually, the best thing to do in this case is just stop trading, analyze what has changed, and then adjust your system and test it in the new environment. Many professionals actually wind up with several systems or variations of a basic system that they can then deploy as conditions change.

As I previously described, it's important to wear the right clothes for the right season or activity. You wouldn't take your parka and snow boots on a vacation to Maui nor would you wear your swim suit on a winter ski vacation.

So go the markets, as well. You have to have the right equipment for the circumstances you're facing.

HOW TO MANAGE DRAWDOWNS

At some point in their careers, all traders will find themselves in a drawdown, a situation where they have lost money and are underwater in their trading. This has happened to everyone I know in this business and most likely it will happen to you as well. If and when that drawdown comes along, how you handle that situation will determine whether or not you'll be a success or failure.

One of the most stressful experiences you can have is losing money. Numerous studies have pointed out that the pain of losing money is much greater than the pleasure associated with making money. It hurts a lot more when you lose.

As humans, we're genetically programmed to survive. We're genetically programmed to avoid pain, and when we encounter pain, we do everything we can to make it stop. When it comes to trading, "making it stop" can take various forms.

Most people will just quit. This isn't usually the best decision because now your losses are permanent. Retail investors do this again and again as they chase from bubble to bubble, get burned, and quit at exactly the wrong time and then chase the next hot investment idea

Some people will take the opposite course and panic and try to "catch up" which leads to excessive risk taking in an effort to get back to break even and recoup their losses. This usually isn't the best course either because the outcome generally is that they'll end up losing even more money than they already have.

Others will just start tinkering with their system or throw it out all together on a search for "the holy grail," hopping from idea to idea and system to system and wind up with no system at all.

People who subscribe to newsletters become what I call "newsletter hoppers" who bounce from system to system and become what editors like myself call "hot money." The only problem with hot money is that it usually ends up becoming lost money.

Most often, none of these responses will result in success. They might make the pain stop for awhile but they almost always will inevitably lead to pain, depression, and failure. The only thing I've found that works when you're in a drawdown is to take the long view. No system is perfect. And your success or failure, your self-worth, isn't dependent on how your system is doing.

The best thing to do, generally speaking, is to take a break, review your system, and if it's still valid, just reenter on a paper trading basis or with small amounts of capital and dip your toe back into the water.

Just like the old saying, "you have to get back on the horse that threw you," the same holds true for active trading. As long as you stay in the game, you have a chance to be a winner. If you quit or get blown out of the game, it's game over and your losing status becomes permanent. That's why all of the subjects we've discussed thus far in this book are so important; they give you a chance to be successful, to avoid blowing yourself up, to help you get back up when you fall down, and to get back in the game and win.

CONCLUSION

It's easy to argue that systems and signals and risk management and stop losses are critical to trading success. But I really believe that the single most important factor that will make or break you is the psychology of trading and how successful you are at managing your emotions and ego.

If you take one thing away from our time together, it is that you must find a style of trading that suits you and then you must have the discipline to follow your system while operating as much as possible in a vacuum. You must trade without emotion and ego.

All the noise and confusion around you are distractions that will lead to your failure. Your human emotion will lead you to failure if you allow it to do so. Mastering yourself is paramount and the cornerstone of any and all success or failure you will experience.

PART VI

Super Sectors: Five "Super Sectors" That Could Change Your Life

I n this section we're going to take a look at five economic, political, and financial sectors that could be leaders going forward over the next three to five years. I've labeled these "super sectors" because I feel they are going to be influenced by enormous financial and geopolitical forces over the next few years.

The winds of change are blowing around the world and investors who can identify sectors and countries that are likely to profit from these changes will very likely have the opportunity to profit as well.

Everyone would like to have the proverbial crystal ball but, unfortunately, none of us do. However, what we can do is judge probabilities based upon the immense global trends that we see unfolding around us.

We'll take a look at some of these "super sectors" in the next few chapters and then we'll hear from other experts in the fields of finance and investment and get their perspectives on what they see ahead for super sectors where extraordinary opportunities might lie.

CHAPTER 15

Super Sector No. 1: The Rise of Asia

M uch has been written about China and its ongoing rise to power, and I feel that China will certainly be a super sector in the coming years.

Additionally, my opinion is that the entire region is going to undergo enormous growth and a rise to prosperity as money flows towards China, potentially transforming countries like Singapore, Vietnam, Malaysia, Taiwan, and South Korea into very high growth areas with robust economies.

Going farther afield, India very likely will be an emerging power-house as well, as this region expands its economic and political sphere of influence.

A CLOSER LOOK AT CHINA

China currently has the world's fastest-growing economy and more than one billion, three hundred million people plunging headlong into capitalism.

I've been to China many times and it reminds me of what the "Wild West" must have been like during the early developmental years of the United States. The Chinese practice an unfettered, almost lawless form of capitalism, with street hustlers and shopkeepers grabbing you by the arm and pulling you into their stalls and not letting go until they sell you something. There is absolutely no respect for intellectual property or copyright and you can buy a "genuine imitation" of almost anything you want, whether it be the latest style in neckties or a new DVD that hasn't even been released yet in the United States.

The country has amazing public buildings. Their airports are dazzling displays of technology and efficiency and their downtowns are showcases of architectural design and wonder. The Shanghai skyline at night looks like Las Vegas on steroids with its dazzling towers and orbs and light shows to amaze the spectators and tourists who float the Huangpu River in front of the well-known and upscale district known as The Bund.

But these modern-looking metropolises are only skin deep, almost like Potemkin Villages, because if you go back just a few blocks into the heart of the cities, you find that this is still very much a Third World country in spite of its headlong rush into the future.

So the question has to be, and it's an important question, is how will this new economic power evolve? Will they develop a broad middle class like the United States and the Western World, or will they look more like other wealthy nations where wealth is centered among the ruling class and the masses remain at significantly reduced standards of living?

Will the Chinese Communist Party be able to retain control or will the people demand political freedom to go along with their newfound economic freedom? Will the central political bosses turn away from capitalism and return to the old ways to maintain control?

I know of no other combination of political dictatorship and economic freedom, and it will be fascinating—and critical—to the world's economy to see if this unique experiment can be successful.

If China stays on its current course and remains committed to a capitalistic economy, there's little doubt that the country is well on its way to becoming the most powerful economy in the world. It's not a matter of "if" but only "when." If they do stay on their current course then other questions will need to be answered, and the answers will undoubtedly have enormous political and economic implications for the entire world.

Will the Yuan become the world's reserve currency? Will the United States become a client state of China, owing our future to this monolith and its willingness to buy up our debt? Politically and militarily, will China be friendly to us and the other countries of the region or will it be a threat?

When you go to China, you're struck by the energy and push and the high level of education among those who have been lucky enough to go to school. You're struck by their drive and ambition to get things like cars that we take for granted and this has resulted in their becoming the world's largest buyers of automobiles.

Assuming that they remain on their current course, we can make some logical predictions of what the future might look like.

Looking out into the near future, there is little question that China will continue to suck up huge amounts of raw materials, energy, and capital in their headlong expansion, and that this growth and demand present enormous opportunities for investors in the coming years. China has become the largest user of steel and cement in the world and with double-digit growth rates, demand for all sorts of raw materials can be expected to continue to rise. Think copper and aluminum, platinum, iron ore, and coal. In each of these areas, China has surpassed the United States as the dominant market.

Shanghai will become the financial center of Asia in the next few years and China's currency could very well replace the dollar as the world reserve currency. Global reserve currencies belong to countries that are creditors, and unfortunately the United States has become the world's largest debtor nation. U.S. creditors like China aren't happy with this situation, for obvious reasons, as the decline of the dollar puts their investments at risk, and so we could see an acceleration of efforts to move the world away from the dollar.

This has already started with rumblings to create some sort of international reserve currency through the International Monetary Fund, a basket of currencies or even a return to a hard asset-backed currency like gold.

There are several unmistakable facts that will give China and Asia more sway over the economic future of the United States. Five out of the top seven holders of U.S. debt are in Asia, led by Japan and China and followed up by South Korea, Taiwan, and Hong Kong. It's not hard to foresee a time where the debtor will have to bow down to the demands of the creditor, much like the old mining worker who "owed his soul to the company store."

As we move through the next few years, we could see an ever-accelerating shift in the balance of the world's economic and financial power away from the United States and the Western World and towards China, in particular, and Asia in general.

THE STORY DOESN'T END WITH CHINA

While China is the 900-pound gorilla in the Asian region, other countries to be reckoned with are South Korea, Malaysia, Singapore, Taiwan, and Vietnam.

South Korea is a Western-like country but with Asian-like work ethic and education, and if you have the chance to go there, you will see a hard working, well-educated, and industrious populous. It's known as the most "wired" country in the world and everyone on the subways has a laptop, cell phone, or iPod—usually all three. Every time I ride the subway in Seoul, I notice its clean, modern cars and safe, well-lit stations crowded with well-dressed people and marvel at the contrast to subway rides I've had in New York City.

The South Korean economy is on a high-growth rate path and many, many South Koreans are pushing hard for reunification of the Korean Peninsula and reforming Korea into one country. After years of neglect and Communist policies, the growth and industrialization that could come from a reunited Korea could be nothing short of staggering.

Turning our attention farther south we find Malaysia, Singapore, and Vietnam. Malaysia has an abundance of raw materials and is a global leader in rubber and palm oil exports along with logging and timber. It also has ample resources of tin, oil, and natural gas, adding muscle to its economic presence in the region.

Singapore has developed into a regional banking center and headquarters for many multinational companies and this gleaming city-state is the world's fourth largest center for foreign exchange trading, in line behind only London, New York, and Tokyo.

Across the South China Sea to the west, Vietnam is one of the world's fastest-growing economies and the third largest producer of oil in Southeast Asia. I can remember flying over Vietnam after the end of the Vietnam War as a young U.S. Air Force pilot, and looking down at their miles and miles of beautiful beaches and tropical jungles and thinking that one day those beaches would be lined with international hotels and resorts; now some 30 years later, that vision is starting to be realized as Vietnam builds up its tourism industry and is rapidly being discovered by the rest of the world.

HOW CAN YOU PARTICIPATE?

It's not within the scope of this book to give investment advice and none of this discussion should be construed to be investment advice or specific recommendations of any kind. However if you look at the big picture, it's easy to see that there are many ways for investors to gain exposure to this region of the world.

The most obvious path would be to participate in one of the many specific country funds that have been established in the ETF universe to represent this region.

Another option is an Exchange Traded Fund that takes a broader view and invests in representative companies from the entire region. Again, there are a number of these available and worthy of your due diligence.

A third option would be to seek out opportunities in the types of things that are going to be in high demand in these areas, things we've discussed like steel, aluminum, copper, and other raw materials.

And finally, individual stocks of companies that have significant business dealings in this region of the world could offer opportunity as well.

CONCLUSION

It's easy to see that Asia and China, in particular, represent a "super sector" that very likely will dominate the course of world economic events for many years to come.

As China moves to the forefront as the world's largest economy, an enormous shift in the balance of global economic power will take place. Throughout history, seismic shifts like this have created enormous profit opportunities for those who are in the "right place at the right time," and there's absolutely no reason to suppose that this time would be any different.

Like the Industrial Revolution or the dawn of the Internet Age, the emergence of China and Asia will change the global investing landscape forever.

I haven't seen any statistics but I'm sure more billionaires will be created along the Pacific Rim over the next ten years than in any other region of the world. With this kind of growth and opportunity, even the most basic retail investors could find opportunity here with a minimal amount of research.

The region comes with massive risks, of course, and high volatility and wild price swings are highly likely to be experienced by those who choose to invest in this highly speculative and dynamic area. Wild price gyrations throughout Asian stock markets have been the norm in recent years and this could likely continue as their violent and unregulated development continues.

Still, investors who are forearmed and forewarned could find Asia brimming with opportunities and excitement as we move forward through the current decade.

CHAPTER 16

Super Sector No. 2: Energy

I t should come as no surprise to anyone that energy would be a super sector going forward for as far as the eye can see. Here we're talking about the entire spectrum of energy to include oil, natural gas, and possible alternative energies that have yet to emerge.

Taking a look at the big picture, the supply/demand equation is very precarious and dangerous, and the economic, political, and social impacts of energy and its pricing and use will be a major factor we'll all be facing on our economic landscape in the future.

As always there will be dangers and opportunities, and the winners will be those who find themselves on the right side of this new and dynamic global equation.

THE BAD NEWS ABOUT SUPPLY

There's little question that global oil supplies have passed their peak and are dwindling. Looking back, most of the new, significant crude oil discoveries were made in the 1960s and most experts agree that global oil production reached its zenith shortly thereafter. New discoveries have been smaller and less productive and nations that have traditionally been oil exporters will become net importers as we go forward through the next few years.

China has become an oil importer, and Mexico, which is one of the largest suppliers of the United States, will cease to be a significant exporter within the next few years. Even the Middle Eastern countries like

Saudi Arabia are forecasting reduced exports as they expand their own economies and internal demand.

Russia, which has vast supplies and is the second largest oil producer in the world, has also seen its peak production in the rear view mirror and so could have less oil available for export in future years than it does today. Major deposits like the Athabasca Oil Sands in Canada hold enormous quantities of oil but these come with a slew of environmental concerns which makes it unlikely that they will be a major contributor over the next few years.

Aside from physical supply concerns, geopolitical affairs are a factor, as well, with much of the world's oil supply centered in less than stable regions like Iran, Iraq, the entire Middle East, Nigeria, Venezuela, and even Russia. It's not hard to envision some sort of political crisis that could almost instantly trigger a global energy supply crisis.

Almost all experts agree that the lights are not going to suddenly go out because we've used up all of the world's oil. We will have oil but that oil will be more expensive and harder to reach and so the "net, net" is that oil supplies will be tighter and countries like the United States very likely will experience adverse consequences from its lack of internal supplies and the long sought after goal of energy independence.

THE BAD NEWS ABOUT DEMAND

The view on the other side of the economic equation of supply and demand is equally grim as we see ever increasing demand for energy coming from all corners of the world.

We've already discussed China's growth curve, and India is right behind. The growth of these two countries alone will severely strain world oil supplies in the coming years. Assuming that the industrialized world recovers from The Great Recession, demand in the Western world will increase as well, along with growth in places like Brazil, Vietnam, and the Middle East.

Demand forecasts are all over the lot, depending upon whom you read, with numbers ranging from single digit rises in demand to as much as 50 to 60 percent over the next two decades. But no matter what the specific numbers turn out to be, common sense tells you that there are going to be ever-increasing claims upon, and competition for, oil as the world's population grows and as the emerging world develops into industrialized economies.

I'm not an economist, but simple rules of supply and demand tell you that it's highly likely that oil prices will rise, and rise substantially and steadily over the next few years.

ECONOMIC, POLITICAL, AND SOCIAL IMPACTS

If we're accurate to say that oil prices will rise, the net outcome depends upon where you sit in the oil supply/demand chain. For importers like the United States, Japan, and the Euro zone, the news will be dismal, while for exporters like the Middle Eastern countries and Russia, the world will be a friendly, happy place and their coffers will be bursting with petrodollars collected from the oil-consuming nations of the world.

The United States imports three quarters of its daily oil needs and is by far the world's largest user of fossil fuels. This puts us in an extraordinarily weak position, both economically and politically. If prices rise, this will further crimp the American economy as so much of our everyday life is tied to oil. Think about what life will be like in your neighborhood with oil prices locked in the triple digit range forever. Higher oil prices will likely translate into higher inflation and less disposable income, because every dollar we put into our gas tanks is one less dollar that we could spend on other items and consumables.

Energy reserves, or lack thereof, could further shift global power away from countries like the United States, Japan, and the Euro zone and towards Russia and the Middle East. In simple terms, the Golden Rule would be at work: "He, who has the gold, makes the rules." Only this time it is black gold and it's very likely the Saudis and Russians, who have the gold, will be making the rules.

The social impacts of rising oil prices could be large and far reaching, both in the United States and around the world. In the United States we could see continued erosion of the middle class as inflation and high oil prices impact disposable incomes and purchasing power.

More extreme scenarios could include domestic social unrest and the most extreme possibilities include increased competition and even "oil wars" among nations for a resource that everyone needs and that could be in short supply. Any kind of oil shock or disruption in supplies could trigger potentially severe international events.

POSSIBLE SOLUTIONS

As always, every problem creates an opportunity, and in our current discussion, solutions rest in alternative energy products to conventional oil supplies. These include things like the oil sands we've previously mentioned, natural gas, coal and so called "clean coal," hydroelectricity, alternative energy sources like solar and wind, and the bedeviled nuclear power industry. Each of these offer potential solutions to the energy supply/demand/cost problem and each could provide potential opportunities to investors in the coming years.

POSSIBLE OUTCOMES

In my opinion, the energy evolution could result in several possible outcomes, each of which offers investors potential opportunity.

The mainstream forecast is for rising energy prices which will lead to higher global inflation, more wealth for the oil producers, and less wealth for consumers. This scenario would point toward more opportunity on the "long" side of the oil pricing equation.

An alternative outcome would be the realization by the United States and the world that issues like dependence on foreign oil, climate change, and dwindling supplies are real hazards to our future, not only economically but even on a basic survival level if the situation continues to deteriorate.

The current situation is not a surprise. I can clearly remember the first Arab oil embargo that began in October 1973 and extended into March 1974.

In December 1973 I had just finished Air Force pilot training and my wife and I were driving cross country to various post graduate training assignments. Because of the Arab oil embargo, we had to plan our gas stops based on an "odd/even" rationing system based on the last number of your license plates. Along our cross country route, many gas stations were closed as they had run out of supplies and those that were open oftentimes had long lines of cars waiting to fill up. Nobody had ever seen anything quite like this, and even way back in those dark ages, feeble attempts at energy independence were made with President Nixon and Henry Kissinger announcing "Project Independence" with the stated goal of making the United States energy independent by 1980.

Of course that never happened because memories are short and human nature, particularly the American form of it, always wants to take the easy way out. But conversely, our survival instinct is strong and it's not hard to imagine a crisis response project much like we saw during World War II when we finally realized that we had to do whatever it took to defeat Nazi Germany.

Many have spoken of a need for a "Manhattan Project" to resolve the nation's energy crisis, and I imagine that is what we will finally see, but only when the situation has become desperate. We're not there yet but it's easy to envision a time in the not too distant future when we could find ourselves with our backs up against the wall in regard to dwindling and endangered energy supplies.

If and when that happens, I think the immediate result would be a renewed and unstoppable push towards nuclear energy. Of all the "alternative" sources, nuclear is by far the most proven and the most rapidly accessible. We only need to look to Europe to see its effectiveness, not to mention the U.S. nuclear submarines and aircraft carriers that ply the world's oceans without incident everyday. The best part of the nuclear solution is that current technology could be quickly implemented and deployed in a crisis situation.

I consider myself an environmentalist, but I have to say that I think the "greens" have it all wrong when it comes to nuclear energy. In my mind, nuclear is a far more environmentally pleasing alternative than fossil fuels. We could have cleaner air, fewer problems with climate change, and at the same time resolve, or at least minimize, the dangers associated with our dependence upon foreign oil.

HOW CAN YOU PARTICIPATE?

There will be numerous ways for investors to participate in the energy super sector over the coming years, some obvious and some not so obvious.

Upfront, of course, there are numerous Exchange Traded Funds that directly track the price of oil and that could be used by investors looking for exposure to the oil market. Commodity futures also offer the potential for profits or losses from the rise or fall in the price of oil and other related products.

One could also look to broader-based energy ETFs and the stocks of oil companies, refiners, and oil service companies. Natural gas ETFs are available as are funds in the alternative energy space of coal, solar, and wind. You can even find an ETF to gain exposure to the nuclear power industry.

A different take on the energy super sector is to go "long" in countries that are net exporters and are likely to profit from the economic and geopolitical shifts we've discussed or to "short" those countries that are likely to come up on the short end of the stick if energy prices continue to rise and supplies remain constrained.

If the United States finds itself in the desperation scenario—which is not as farfetched as it seems—being "long" in nuclear power could be a very comforting place to be.

CONCLUSION

Everyone seems to agree that energy will be a major factor on the world's political, economic, and military landscape for many years to come, maybe forever. Its strategic importance and the seismic dynamics of supply and demand will create enormous shifts in opportunities and centers of power as these forces play out against one another.

Big trends like this always offer unusual opportunities, as well as risk, and for investors who can make a careful analysis of the situation, potentially large rewards could be realized.

CHAPTER 17

Super Sector No. 3: Health Care

H ealth care is a constant subject of debate in America, and for good reason, as it's a major cause of economic stress for individuals, corporations, and governments.

As I write this, President Obama and Congress are wrestling with the latest version of a national health plan and this debate is bound to continue as we move into the future and our population continues to age.

But like every other problem, there is always an associated opportunity and that's why Super Sector No. 3 is Health Care.

THE AGING BABY BOOMERS

The Baby Boom Generation could almost be considered a super sector all by itself. Ever since coming on the scene in 1946 after the end of World War II, the baby boom has been the "rabbit in the python," the enormous and influential demographic bulge moving through the pipeline of American society.

Having been born in 1950, I'm at the leading edge of the baby boom, and as the baby boom generation progressed through the various stages of its life cycle, enormous demand was created which in turn created enormous profit and investment opportunities.

In the 1950s, we were responsible for massive sales of diapers and baby food, then the construction of schools and the development of suburbia, and later, significant growth in higher education. We fueled the housing boom that lasted through the 1980s and 1990s and the stock market booms of the 1980s, 1990s, and 2000s. Following that, we escalated the prices of second homes.

Now as we come to our retirement years and old age, it's quite predictable that we will continue functioning as a "super sector," spiking demand for health care, pharmaceutical products, physical therapy, managed care, hospital visits, and Alzheimer's care. Finally, the funeral home industry is facing twenty years of bullish demand!

In 2006, the first baby boomers turned 60 years old and in 2011, the leading edge will reach the magic retirement age of 65. There are more than 78 million people in the baby boom and more than 7,000 turn age sixty every day, approximately 330 every hour!

BABY BOOMERS AND THE COST OF HEALTH CARE

In 2004, according to the U.S. Bureau of Labor Statistics, the average annual expenditure on health care for people aged 45 to 54, the center of the baby boom, was $2,695. As people age, this number rises significantly and for people ages 55 to 64, the average annual number is $3,262 and for over age 65, it goes up to $3,899.

Since most of the baby boom is in good health and has benefited from exercise and quality medical care for their entire lives, their life spans will very likely be longer and many baby boomers can be reasonably looking forward to living twenty years or more past traditional retirement age.

When Social Security was created in 1935, average life expectancy was 59 while today it's 82 for a 65-year old male and nearly 85 for a 65-year old female, according to the U.S. Census Bureau, and forecast to continue increasing. This extra longevity has enormous implications for Medicare and Social Security, as well as the cost of health care, because it has been conclusively proven that health care spending increases dramatically as people age.

GROWTH IN NATIONAL HEALTH CARE EXPENDITURES

According to the U.S. Department of Health and Human Services, national spending on health care is forecast to grow at an average of 6.2 percent per year from now until 2018. This will most likely outpace the average growth of the economy over the same time period and grow from $2.4 trillion in

2008 to $4.4 trillion in 2018—or a nearly 85 percent increase—and account for 20.3 percent of Gross Domestic Product.

According to a study by McKinsey and Company, "in 2006 the U.S. spent $2.1 trillion on health care, more than twice what the nation spent on food and more than China's citizens consumed on all goods and services."[1] Growth in prescription drug demand will also continue to grow as Medicare now covers those services, and the price of new and ever more expensive technologies will also add to the increased cost of health care.

Finally, as we age, we will become more disease ridden as a country with a higher incidence of chronic illness and expensive diseases like cancer and Alzheimer's.

POSSIBLE SOLUTIONS AND OUTCOMES

Unfortunately there's no solution to growing old and dying unless someone comes up with the Fountain of Youth sometime in the near future. In fact, the most likely outcome is that technology will continue to find ways to extend the human lifespan which will actually make the problem even worse than current projections anticipate. We'll most likely have more people living longer and so there will be a steady and unrelenting increase in demand for health care.

Therefore, overall spending and expenses could be far higher than projected today as the old laws of supply and demand kick in like they always do. With more old people living longer, there will be increased demand on all forms of health care. Plus, several other factors are conspiring to push prices ever higher.

THE EVER-GROWING MEDICAL MONSTER

Even if Congress and the President ever mustered up the courage to try to tackle the rising cost of health care or cut Medicare benefits, it would be political suicide because elderly people tend to be high probability voters and the likelihood of them (us) going along with any sort of cuts to Medicare is unlikely. The elderly are going to be expensive on the health care front and demand the best, or at least, unfettered access to quality health care.

Don't forget that this is the baby boom generation we're talking about and it's very likely that they will approach aging with the same zeal and rebellious nature they have demonstrated throughout their life spans. In just a few years, I believe that the same people who marched on Washington,

D.C. in protest of the Vietnam War will be back again, this time lobbying and protesting against any proposed cuts to Medicare or Social Security benefits.

On the supply side, the medical establishment has significant financial incentive to continue delivering high-priced services. Another lab or diagnostic test, whether it's needed or not, can help reduce their exposure to liability insurance claims and adds incremental revenue to their bottom line, so who can blame a doctor or hospital for ordering up a "complete" battery of tests, whether they're absolutely needed or not?

As I write this, "Obama Care" is being wrestled with in Congress, and however this debate turns out, it is nearly certain that there will be increased demand for health care services as more and more people gain access to some sort of national health insurance. It's a lot easier to go to the doctor when you don't have to foot the bill, or at least part of it, and studies prove that richer countries have higher health care bills than poorer ones because they can afford it. Whatever form the final national health insurance package might take, it seems certain that the outcome will be more customers for health care and so more demand and consequently higher prices.

HOW CAN YOU PARTICIPATE?

This is a good question and the answer is simple. Average retail investors already have a wide variety of Exchange Traded Funds available that focus on the health care sector.

Today you can find highly liquid funds that track the Dow Jones U.S. Health Care Index and you can also buy ETFs that invest in baskets of stocks from the biggest health care companies and providers. You can also find ETFs that will get you exposure to pharmaceutical companies and you can get as specialized as investing in ETFs that focus on specialized subsectors of the health care field like Biotech and Genomes.

One can only begin to imagine what new ETFs will come to market as health care becomes a monster and a super sector that's on everybody's radar.

CONCLUSION

Like all of the other super sectors we're talking about, health care is a widespread "mega trend" that will ripple into every corner of American life and have widespread ramifications for every American. If you're old, you will want to have at least reasonable access to health care and if you're young, chances are that you'll be paying higher taxes to fund your parents' ever-growing health care needs.

It's unlikely that any force on the horizon today could derail the medical care monster and stop the rapid growth of this industry. Rather, it's more likely that growth will outstrip current projections rather than somehow be restrained. Americans have never been very good at self-denial and any restrictions on what is seen as a "right" are unlikely.

The most likely scenario calls for continued rapid growth in the cost and demand of all health care, ranging from pharmaceutical products to treatment for disease, hospital services, and long-term care.

With ever increasing demand filling its sails, Super Sector No. 3, Healthcare, is a sector worth recognizing and studying for future investment opportunities.

CHAPTER 18

Super Sector No. 4: Technology

U nless you've been living in a cave for the past ten years, you know that technology and its growth have been the big economic and social story of our times.

From the dawn of the personal computer in Steven Jobs's garage to the iPhone, we have seen literally centuries of progress made in just the span of a few years.

I'm old enough to remember the dawn of television, the first transistor radios, and digital watches, and the progress since those "Leave It to Beaver" days has been nothing short of breathtaking.

There can be no question that technology has been more than the equivalent of the Industrial Revolution and that Bill Gates and Michael Dell and Larry Ellison are the Rockefellers, Carnegies, and Mellons of our day. The personal computer, Internet and smart phones are the equivalent of the steam engine, the Model T, and the assembly line, and, like then, many fortunes have been made in recent years on these emerging technologies.

While some say that all the big money has been made and that the pace of change and innovation has to slow down, I believe that we're still in the very early days of the "Technology Revolution" and that many more opportunities still lie ahead.

A CONNECTED WORLD

Without a doubt, the Internet has been the most disruptive technology ever invented. In just a couple of decades it has completely transformed the way we live and work and has delivered enormous economic and productivity gains to countries around the world.

Think about how much your own life has changed in the last ten years because of the Internet. Now we shop online and work online. Entire industries have been created since the advent of the Internet while whole other industries have been destroyed.

When was the last time you called your stock broker to place a trade or called a travel agent to book an airline ticket? If you have kids, I can be 99 percent certain that they have a Facebook wall and spend an obnoxious amount of time on their cell phones texting their friends.

While you might suppose that the United States is the leader in broadband accessibility, we're actually number 15 among the 30 leading industrialized nations of the world with 26 percent of inhabitants having broadband access compared to 32.8 percent in South Korea, 38 percent in the Netherlands and 37 percent in Denmark, according to the Organization for Economic Co-Operation and Development.

Of course now broadband has gone wireless, and mobile and wireless growth forecasts are equally impressive. In North America in 2007, there were 2.6 million WiFi users and that number is forecast to explode to 14.79 million by 2011, according to the WiMax Forum's forecasts from 2007–2012.

Looking to worldwide Internet usage and growth rates we find the following information from internetworldstats.com:

- In 2009, China had more broadband users than any other country in the world on an absolute basis with 360,000,000 users or 26.9 percent of their population and 20.8 percent of total world users compared to the U.S. with 227,719,000 users or 74.1 percent of the U.S. population and 13.1 percent of users in the world. http://www.internetworldstats.com/top20.htm
- The U.S. growth rate of Internet users from 2000–2009 was 138.8 percent while China's was 1,500 percent, India's was 1,520 percent, Brazil 1,250 percent, and Russia 1,359 percent. Among leading nations, Korea is the "most wired" while Japan, the United Kingdom, and the United States and France round out the top five in terms of overall Internet access and use. http://www.internetworldstats.com/top20.htm

However, from the growth rates it's clear that it won't be long until China, already with the largest percentage of world users, will pull even farther away and many of the developing nations will also be closing the information gap. Of course this translates into enormous growth opportunities for U.S. technology companies as the Information Highway continues to lay down its tracks across the emerging world.

HIGHWAYS IN THE SKY

Man's journey has always been about communication and transportation. Cities like St. Louis that were built along rivers dominated the American landscape until the railroads linked America together, and when the Interstate Highway System was built, cities along the high-speed freeways thrived while those on the old U.S. highway system wilted as traffic was diverted around them.

Today's interstate highway is comprised of broadband, mobile data, and voice communication, and countries, cities, and societies that are wired will thrive while those that aren't will be left behind.

A few years ago, my family and I took a cross-country road trip in our R.V. and traveled from coast to coast and back. One of our stops was Fort Laramie, Wyoming, an old Army fort situated along the route of the Oregon Trail. Early pioneers traveled through here on their way to Oregon in the 1850s and then the Pony Express riders stopped here along their 1,800 mile ride from St. Joseph, Missouri to Sacramento, California.

In 1861, the transcontinental telegraph line, "the talking wire," was laid through the fort as digital connectivity connected the country and the Pony Express ceased operations. The fort itself was bypassed by the transcontinental railroad which was built to the south near Cheyenne, and then Interstate 80 was built, closely tracking the old cross-country routes of the Oregon Trail and Transcontinental Railroad.

My family and I walked the grounds of old Fort Laramie at sunset and as I looked up to see the pink jet trails of an airliner flying overhead, I thought of man's evolution along this route from Pony Express to telegraph to railroad, the interstate system, jet airways, and now cell phone towers and WiFi all connecting us together in different ways during different times of our history.

Communications and transportation have brought birth and death to cities, nations, and regions, and the same cycle of life and death will be at work today and tomorrow as we plunge deeper into the age of wireless broadband and global universal communications.

Today we're entering the age of smart phones, and already approximately 50 percent of cell phone users have smart phones. There's no doubt that in just a short time, 100 percent of cell phone users will be wired with smart phone technology and the growth of "apps" and developments like

Twitter are just in their infancy and that all of these things will offer enormous investment opportunities for people able to recognize the future before it arrives.

EMERGING TECHNOLOGIES

While the internet gets the lion's share of the press, scores of other emerging technologies are developing at light speed and these could offer the same or greater potential in the years going forward.

Looking just a few years down the road we can predict with some certainty that we'll see breakthroughs in areas like nuclear fusion, hydrogen power, and biofuels. Electric cars are already here and will continue to be a more dominant factor in the automotive industry while machine learning and quantum computing will continue the dizzying growth and evolution of the computer industry.

In the last chapter we discussed health care, and clearly this field will undergo a sea change as genetic engineering, stem cell research and new cures for chronic disease emerge.

Finally, we'll truly be entering a world that in my youth could only be described as science fiction with robotics, nanotechnology, and artificial intelligence playing increasingly important and dominant roles in our lives.

On the leading edge of this futuristic thinking is Ray Kurzweil, who has been the recipient of the $500,000 MIT-Lemelson Prize, the world's biggest award for innovation, and the National Medal of Technology, the highest honor for technology awarded by the United States. Kruzweil says that technological change is "exponential, contrary to the common-sense 'intuitive linear' view. So we won't experience 100 years of progress in the 21st century—it will be more like 20,000 years."[1]

To my limited brain, change equals opportunity and Super Sector No. 4: Technology, should be an arena of enormous opportunity as we enter the second decade of the 21st century.

HOW CAN YOU PARTICIPATE?

For more than a decade, technology stocks have been market leaders and the cause of enormous booms and busts through the Tech Wreck of 2000 and The Great Recession. Once confined to the NASDAQ and OTC Exchanges, tech stocks today have wide representation on the S&P 500. Even the venerable Dow Jones Industrials sport the presence of Cisco, Hewlett Packard, IBM, Intel, Microsoft, and United Technologies.

The tech sector has been a perennial market leader in recent years, and all expectations are that this reign should continue.

Companies like Google and Amazon are household names while iPhones spring up seemingly everywhere. Not to be outdone, Blackberries or "Crackberries" as they're sometimes affectionately known, fill the hands of many a busy executive and old stalwarts like Hewlett Packard and IBM still go nose to nose with "newcomers" like Dell and Apple.

Looking ahead, enormous opportunities loom in almost every nook and cranny of technology. Whether it is software, hardware, semiconductors, or broadband, companies are forecasting and planning for robust growth over the next ten years.

The reasons for this growth are simple and go back to our earlier super sector discussions. The emerging world will very likely drive exponential growth in technology, and we in the developed world will do our share to fuel further growth with ongoing developments in health care and energy infrastructure.

For us as investors, once again, Exchange Traded Funds offer an almost unlimited array of investment possibilities. We can easily get exposure to general technology funds, semiconductors, software, hardware, or broadband and we can just as easily gain investment exposure in subsectors like biotech and nanotechnology.

The ride won't be straight up and it won't necessarily be easy, but for investors and traders with just the simplest systems, the potential could be enormous. Plus, with Exchange Traded Funds, you don't have to pick the next Apple or Microsoft because quite likely you'll already find it residing in one of the ETFs that you might choose.

CONCLUSION

Who among us could survive without our Internet connection or cell phone? When times get tough, we can cut back on dining out or taking a vacation, but if your laptop or cell phone dies, you have to replace them virtually on that very day.

Technology has gone from being an odd novelty to necessity, a staple of our personal and business lives, and so while competition will remain steep, opportunities likely will abound as ever more sophisticated new developments continue popping up around us.

Super Sector No. 4: Technology, looms as an overriding player on the investing landscape for the next five to ten years and beyond.

CHAPTER 19

Super Sector No. 5: Financials

The Great Recession has brought unprecedented, and some would even say cataclysmic change to the world's financial landscape. Major U.S. banks have disappeared or merged; powerful brokerages have been absorbed or tossed onto the "dustbin of history," as Leon Trotsky so eloquently put it in 1917. In the United States, the national government has inserted itself into the functioning of private enterprise and the financial sector in a way that has never been previously experienced.

The historic intervention by global central banks to avert a worldwide depression has immeasurably changed the functioning of the world's financial system and all of these factors combined will very likely result in both unprecedented and unusual dangers and opportunities as the global financial system reacts to these historic measures.

We're going to take a look at the financial sector itself and then focus on several financial subsectors that could be super sectors in the next few years.

THE FINANCIAL SECTOR

As I write this in late December, 2009, (XLF) the Select Sector Financial SPDR, is widely viewed as a proxy for the U.S. Financial Sector.

Top ten holdings today include:

1. JP Morgan Chase and Co.
2. Bank of America Corp.
3. Wells Fargo and Co.
4. Goldman Sachs Group
5. Citigroup, Inc.
6. American Express Co.
7. U.S. Bancorp
8. Morgan Stanley
9. Bank of New York Mellon Corp.
10. MetLife, Inc.

The list is clearly an impressive compilation of the bedrock of the U.S. financial system and nearly every one of these institutions was severely rocked by the cataclysmic events of The Great Recession.

XLF peaked in 2007 in the high $30s/share range, then tumbled into the $8/share range during the Bear Market of 2008–2009, and as I write this, has clawed its way back to the mid $14/share range, approximately 40 percent below its former highs.

Through The Great Recession, the money center banks, investment banks, and insurance companies suffered a near death experience and were put on life support by the Federal Reserve and U.S. Treasury through an unprecedented array of bailouts and life saving measures designed to stave off a systemic banking collapse and ensuing Depression.

Clearly we were on the edge of Armageddon and the only thing that separated The Great Recession from The Great Depression was that these banks remained open, people could access their money, and global confidence in the central banking system's power and the government's credibility remained in place. It seems to have worked as the nation's and world's economy slowly emerges from the worst downturn that anyone has ever seen since the 1930s.

Still today, banks aren't lending, credit is tight, the consumer is deleveraging, real estate foreclosures continue to be problematic, and delinquent loans remain at historically high levels.

So while XLF has had an almost 80 percent bounce from its lows in March 2009, no one could say that the Financial Industry is yet healthy or that banking, lending, insurance, or financial services have yet returned to any kind of norm. The U.S. government has made it clear that many members of XLF are "too big to fail," in spite of their immense problems, and so it would seem that this sector could offer some excellent opportunities going forward.

WARREN BUFFETTOLOGY

Warren Buffett's philosophy is, "We simply attempt to be fearful when others are greedy and to be greedy only when others are fearful,"[1] and that strategy could well apply to the financial sector today and for several years ahead.

As I said a moment ago, this sector has suffered a near death experience and in November 2009, stands near frozen like the proverbial deer in the headlights as it tries to figure out where to go from here.

Is there another shoe to drop? Is there another boogeyman about to jump out of the closet or will it be clear sailing into the future?

I don't have a crystal ball and none of the following is investment advice or recommendations for any particular security, but I think a couple of things are worth noting from an academic point of view.

First, our government has openly stated that these banks are too big to fail and so it would seem that XLF and its larger members very likely could have become virtually risk-free investments as the full faith and credit of the U.S. government now stand behind them. There are several types of risk when one considers making an investment; market risk, company risk, industry-specific risk, among others, and effectively the government very well may have removed company and industry-specific risk from the financial sector or at least from its larger members. Of course the government could always take away this implied "guarantee" but for now it remains in place.

Secondly, to take a page from "Buffettology," it's always a good idea to buy low and sell high, to look for value and buy things when nobody else wants them. In this sector we have a major global bank like Citigroup currently selling in the $3/share range, down from the mid $50s, and Bank of America selling in the mid-teens, down from the mid $50s, while many other members of XLF are selling at discounts of 30 to 40 percent off their highs. In other words, the Financial Sector is currently on sale.

Of course no one knows if these companies' shares will ever retrace their way to the old highs and resume their lofty positions of former glory or what price they might be when you're reading this book. After the Tech Wreck, many high fliers of that era were "on sale" and they've remained on sale ever since. However, somehow, global banking seems different to me than some high-flying tech startup that never had any revenues or even an established market to start with and that was just powered higher on the strength of a huge, all encompassing bubble.

As the old saying goes, "money makes the world go 'round," and so it's logical to conclude that, sometime and somehow, it's a good possibility that these banks are going to get back in the business of banking and that we will find some kind of new normalcy, that the economy would eventually recover and start growing again. If and when that happens, the financial sector could and should once again become an engine of growth and profitability in the world's economy.

Crafty, old Buffett must see some potential as well, because he already made his bet back in early 2009 when he said that Wells Fargo was healthy and made a substantial purchase. As of September 30, 2009, Warren's company owns more than $8 billion of Wells Fargo stock along with significant holdings in U.S. Bancorp, American Express, Bank of America, M&T BancCorp, SunTrust Banks, The Travelers Companies, and Wesco Financial Corp.

Comparing Buffett's holdings to the major holdings of XLF reveals some remarkable similarities. Considering that this guy is the second richest man in the world, one has to ask if he knows something that the rest of the world doesn't.

THE DOLLAR AND GLOBAL CURRENCY MARKETS

The Forex Market, or global foreign exchange market, is the largest financial market in the world, several multiples bigger than the New York Stock Exchange, the world's largest equity market.

The currency markets have been absolutely roiled by the financial upheavals of 2008–2009 as central banks around the world pumped trillions of dollars into the global financial system. The value of the U.S. dollar plunged during most of 2009 and many experts are calling for the complete demise and collapse of the dollar in coming years as the United States struggles with its debt burden.

Also, during The Great Recession, the Federal Reserve flooded the world's financial system with dollars and ran the printing presses overtime with "quantitative easing." Like always, large supplies of any commodity, dollars included, creates falling prices.

On the other side of the ledger, dollar bulls say the U.S. dollar is still the safe haven currency and that when times get tough, the dollar is the only safe place to be. Meanwhile, hard money advocates say that no "fiat" currency is worth the paper it's printed on and so the only true money is gold and that someday everybody will wake up and realize that and the world will return to a gold standard.

Wherever you stand in this debate, there is little question that the world currency markets will continue to be volatile and provide ample trading and investment opportunities for astute and well-prepared participants.

Strong currencies generally go with creditor nations, net exporters, and strong economies and so it's hard to make a long-term case for a strong dollar. However, I've always said that one should never underestimate the strength, resilience, and size of the U.S. economy.

Other currencies like the Euro and Yuan will compete with the dollar and the volatile foreign exchanges markets are unlikely to settle down anytime soon. This situation makes for ample investment and trading opportunities and so currencies will very likely be a super sector going forward through the next few years.

INTEREST RATES

Interest rates are another financial instrument that has been dramatically affected by the actions of central banks around the world in response to the Great Recession.

With interest rates at virtually zero at the time of this writing, it seems logical that the only way interest rates can go is up. We have been in an unusually long period of low interest rates, dating back to just after the Paul Volker years of 20 percent rates in the early 1980s. Today many experts, both fundamental and technical, are calling for a long-term reversal in interest rates and forecast that we're about to enter a prolonged period of rising interest rates.

The arguments for this position are quite compelling in that the United States will have to finance record amounts of debt and so interest rates will naturally have to rise to attract sufficient buying interest for our paper.

Also, it is argued that the vast quantities of money that have been printed will inevitably lead to higher inflation, which, in turn, will lead to higher interest rates, and many technicians say that the bull market in Treasuries and bonds is over and a long, secular bear market is about to begin.

PRECIOUS METALS

I'm not a gold bug but it's hard to argue that inflation won't be a problem somewhere down the road as the world economy recovers and global growth returns, along with the impacts of the enormous liquidity injected into the system over the past couple of years. Gold bugs call for almost unimaginable levels in the price of gold, some as high as $5-6,000/oz., but looking at the price of gold in a widely accepted scenario of rising inflation and a declining dollar, it's easy to argue that the stage is set for rising precious metals prices.

On the other side of the argument, if financial catastrophe and a "Great Depression 2.0" are in our future, metals most likely will prove to be a store of wealth as they always have during financial crises throughout history.

Beyond factors like inflation and declining currency values, the rest of the world seems to have caught "gold fever" to one extent or other. Central banks are buying gold, particularly China, and the Chinese have even encouraged their citizens to buy gold and silver to protect their savings from currency and stock market fluctuations. If we put 1.3 billion buyers into any market, the laws of supply and demand would imply sharply rising prices.

HOW CAN YOU PARTICIPATE?

Any of the trading systems we've looked at in this book could easily be adapted to the financial markets including interest rates, currencies, and precious metals.

Also, as with the other super sectors, the advent of Exchange Traded Funds has introduced many ETF opportunities for participating in these markets. There are precious metals ETFs, currency ETFs, and ETFs that let you track price changes in both rising and falling interest rate environments. ETFs combined with a successful timing or trading system offer investors unique opportunities not previously available in the financial arena and all of its subsectors.

CONCLUSION

Unlike the previous super sectors we've discussed, financials are a varied but inextricably linked group. They're subject to wild fluctuations caused by government actions and speculation, and it's highly unlikely that they would all appreciate in value at the same time.

If the dollar gets stronger, precious metals would likely weaken. If interest rates rise, bonds would decline (or crash as the doomsayers predict) while the dollar would go up. Bubbles can easily be formed in the precious metals markets because they're relatively smaller than most markets and so prices can make extreme, parabolic moves that require adroit skills to successfully navigate.

Looking ahead, the most likely scenarios would be that any or all of these "sub-super sectors" could have their day in the sun. Therefore these markets would be particularly well suited for short-term traders and practitioners of sector rotation methodologies as well as for investors with short- to medium-time horizons and adequate trend-following tools.

A famous old quotation widely attributed to legendary financier J.P. Morgan, says, "prices will fluctuate" and that fact offers both opportunities and hazards for Super Sector No. 5.

CHAPTER 20

Ask the Experts

*Insights and Advice from
Today's Top Investors, Traders
and Managers*

I n this section, we'll talk with a number of investment and economic experts to get their opinions and outlooks about the economic and investment climate going forward and their view of what areas of the investment world might be "super sectors," that is, investment sectors that have the potential to significantly outperform the general stock market indexes.

These experts are presented alphabetically and I think you'll find their insights both fascinating and informative:

LARRY CONNORS

Mr. Connors is CEO and Co-Founder of Tradingmarkets.com, a leading financial internet web site has over 28 years experience working in the financial markets industry. He started his career in 1982 at Merrill Lynch and later moved on to become a Vice President with Donaldson, Lufkin and Jenrette. Mr. Connors has authored top-selling books on market strategies and volatility trading, including *How Markets Really Work, Short Term Trading Strategies That Work* and *Street Smarts* (with Linda Raschke). *Street Smarts* was selected by *Technical Analysis of Stocks and Commodities* magazine as one of "The Classics" for trading books written in the past century. His latest book, *High Probability ETF Trading: 7 Professional Strategies to Improve Your ETF Trading*, was released in June 2009 and is already in its second printing. *High Probability ETF*

Trading was recently chosen as one of the 10 Best Trading and Investing Book of 2009 by *SFO Magazine.*

John Nyaradi: Could you discuss your views of active management versus buy and hold?

Larry Conners: My views on this topic are pretty much in-line with a growing number of professionals in the industry. The weakness of buy and hold is that in times, for example years like 2000–2002 and in 2008, when bear markets hit, the declines can be pretty severe. And, ultimately, it takes people quite some time to make their money back.

    If you take a look at the number of investors and funds who invested in a number of Nasdaq companies back in 2000, 2001, and 2002, it's now 2010 and they have not earned their money back in many of those investments. It's also going to take many years for those who lost money in 2008 to earn back the 30, 35, 40 percent that money managers lost for them.

    So, in my opinion, and this opinion is obviously ingrained in me and ties into our background, active management is superior to buy and hold. This is especially true if someone is using a consistent approach—and in our case we use model-driven, quantified strategies—they have the potential to do better for example than someone who is using buy and hold and is ultimately susceptible to the bear market years.

John Nyaradi: Do you use technical indicators and which ones do you find to be most effective?

Larry Conners: Yes, we do use technical indicators. They are at the forefront of what we do.

    Pretty much everything we do is quantified, so we will not use any indicators that we cannot quantify. And when we quantify the indicators, we'll look back as short as 10 years to as long as 50 years in the S&P, for example, and with the Dow we'll go back up to 100 years.

    The two indicators that historically have the best edges—especially when they are combined—are the 200-day moving average and the Relative Strength Index (RSI).

    The 200-day moving average tends to draw the line between a bull market and a bear market. Ideally, we want to be buying stocks and ETFs that are above the 200-day moving average, and ideally avoiding or even shorting stocks and ETFs that are below the 200-day moving average.

    You'll see statistically that the 200-day ma has held up very well—especially when you combine it with the 2-period RSI.

Welles Wilder created the Relative Strength Index (RSI) indicator back in the 1970s. It was a brilliant discovery. When he published it, he used a 14-period time frame.

What we've found is that there is no statistical evidence that the 14-period RSI has any edge. But when you start looking at shorter periods, especially a 2-period RSI, you'll see that historically there are quantified edges in both stocks and ETFs.

You're looking for the 2-period RSI to reach extreme low levels before buying—ideally when the stock or ETF is above the 200-day moving average. And you'll want to be locking in profits or at least exiting positions after the 2-period RSI has moved up. This means you're buying into a statistically valid pullback and exiting into strength.

Put those two together and you'll see some wonderful test results, especially with equities and ETFs.

John Nyaradi: What's your view for the U.S. and global economy over the next three to five years? What macroeconomic trends are we facing?

Larry Conners: I'm not qualified to answer that question. I certainly have my own opinions. But my opinions are no better than anyone else who has opinions on it. The optimist in me though is never going to bet against the U.S long-term.

John Nyaradi: What opportunities for investors/traders do you see over the next 3, 5, 10 years?

Larry Conners: I certainly see the opportunity to be able to do more and more active management. The brokerage houses have done a wonderful job in providing tools for research and doing quantified studies. The exchanges have done a tremendous job in bringing out products that allow individuals to manage their own money. And now we are seeing this on a global basis.

Also the tools that allow traders to backtest and see historical results are now in place. This is better than taking someone's opinion and not knowing whether or not there is any evidence that at least a historical edge is in place.

So there are a number of wonderful opportunities that are now available. The fact that commissions have gone to rock bottom prices also allows for wonderful opportunities for people to actively manage their own money.

John Nyaradi: What traps and dangers do you see for investors/traders over the next 3, 5, 10 years?

Larry Conners: I think that potentially some of the traps and dangers that exist today will always be there—especially coming from the financial media.

They tend to promote extremes and a lot of people who tend to be loud and have strong opinions seem to get the attention. At the end of the day, I think potentially all of us can be influenced by that. So that's always been a danger and will likely remain so.

Ideally this is where model-driven trading and statistical trading comes in. If you let the statistics guide you, you're probably going to be better off as opposed to listening to someone coming on television one day saying "Up!" and then a couple of minutes later someone is coming on television and saying "Down!"

So that trap is inherent. It's especially been like this in recent years. And I sense that it will potentially get worse over the next couple of years because it's a very profitable game for the networks. The business programs are very profitable for the networks.

With that said, I do see the opportunities being greater than the traps and dangers. There are always traps and dangers out there. But the opportunities, as I've mentioned earlier, are certainly something I'm looking forward to.

John Nyaradi: What sectors do you see holding the most potential for gains over the next 1 to 3 years, sectors that could be "super sectors?"

Larry Conners: When we look at markets, we do everything on a short term basis. We're usually in positions for, on average, 3 to 7 days with the majority of our position trading. So we're not looking out over 1 to 3 years.

What I do see over the next 1 to 3 years is that more and more trading products will be brought to the market. New ETF products especially will become bigger. The exchanges and fund sponsors will continue to bring out products, and also insurance type products that will allow people to protect their portfolios.

We see that now the options markets have gotten bigger and bigger—options are a form of insurance. You see that the VIX products, the volatility products that have come on market have become very popular. I see that becoming bigger and bigger, and that gives all of us the opportunity to create portfolios and to have the proper tools to hedge and protect our portfolios over time.

For the past three years we've been building a software program that allows professional traders to see the edges of every liquid stock that trades in the U.S. and these edges are updated every 20 seconds. The traders can also quickly build customized portfolios based upon historical edges that have existed for more than a decade. This software product can be found at www.themachineus.com.

John Nyaradi: Anything else you'd like to add?

Larry Conners: The main thing I'd like to add is the fact that the more you can quantify behavior, the more you can quantify your strategy, the stronger you are going to be.

We see this with many of our customers over the years. And now with the brokerage houses making these tools available, the more you quantify your strategies the better you'll be able to put together high performing portfolios.

Those are important things. And the more effort you put into it, the greater your results are likely to be for years to come.

DR. MARC FABER

Dr. Marc Faber was born in Zurich, Switzerland. He went to school in Geneva and Zurich and finished high school with the Matura. He studied Economics at the University of Zurich and, at the age of 24, obtained a PhD in Economics, magna cum laude.

Between 1970 and 1978, Dr. Faber worked for White Weld & Company Limited in New York, Zurich, and Hong Kong. Since 1973, he has lived in Hong Kong. From 1978 to February 1990, he was the Managing Director of Drexel Burnham Lambert (HK) Ltd. In June 1990, he set up his own business, Marc Faber Limited, which acts as an investment advisor and fund manager.

Dr. Faber publishes a widely read monthly investment newsletter "The Gloom Boom & Doom Report" which highlights unusual investment opportunities, and is the author of several books including *Tomorrow's Gold: Asia's Age of Discovery* which was first published in 2002 and highlights future investment opportunities around the world. *Tomorrow's Gold* was on Amazon's bestseller list for several weeks and is being translated into Japanese, Chinese, Korean, Thai, and German.

Dr. Faber is also a regular contributor to several leading financial publications around the world. A book about Dr. Faber, *Riding the Millennial Storm*, by Nury Vittachi, was published in 1998. A regular speaker at various investment seminars, Dr. Faber is well-known for his "contrarian" investment approach. He is also associated with a variety of funds and is a member of the Board of Directors of numerous companies.

John Nyaradi: Dr. Faber, what sectors do you see leading the way over the next three to five years?

Dr. Marc Faber: Commodities should be relatively attractive provided the global economy recovers. Commodity cycles tend to last from peak to peak 45 to 60 years and basically we're in the ninth year of a commodity bull market. In a normal global economic environment, prices should continue to go up.

John Nyaradi: What is your outlook for the price of gold and silver over the next three to five years? How about oil?

Dr. Marc Faber: Obviously gold has outperformed other assets since 1999. It's up four times from its low but had a huge bear market from 1980 to 1999. This is the ninth year of a bull market. Gold is not widely held and my impression from the emails I get is that most people have already sold their gold. So there's an underinvestment in gold and it can continue to go up. Central banks will continue to print money. If they don't, there will be massive defaults. Even in a deflationary environment, gold could do relatively well.

John Nyaradi: What's your view for the U.S. and global economy over the next three to five years?

Dr. Marc Faber: It's conceivable that we will have a short recovery but I don't think it will be sustainable. Government debt will be a big issue; we could see corporate defaults as well as sovereign defaults. We had a boom from 2001 to 2007 and I think it's unlikely we will get back to those levels for the next five years.

John Nyaradi: What opportunities for investors do you see over the next three to five years?

Dr. Marc Faber: Commodities. If inflation is defined as an increase in the quantity of money and debt, the cost of replacement will increase and so companies that have assets in basic industries will be relatively attractive. Globally, insurance is also quite attractive. New technologies like nanotechnology, biotech, hi-tech—in those areas there are opportunities but you need to have a specialist to determine the winners.

John Nyaradi: What dangers do you see for investors over the next three to five years?

Dr. Marc Faber: The retail investor got killed in 2000, then missed most of the bull market in commodities, got involved in real estate and got burned again, then speculated in commodities but came in late in the game. The retail investor is in bad shape and isn't in a position to participate meaningfully in the bull market.

In 2009, he rushed into bond funds and shunned equities and missed the bull market in equities. In 2010 and 2011, he will rush back into equities at the wrong time. The individual should adopt a much more disciplined and diversified approach. Individuals always become absolutely convinced of something and put all their money into it, like the NASDAQ during the tech bubble. The individual has to learn to have a strategy and diversification and should consider the risk of every investment before considering the profit.

John Nyaradi: Could you discuss your outlook for China and Asia over the next three to five years?

Dr. Marc Faber: Some people think it's a Dubai only a thousand times larger. But I don't believe that. If someone looks at China, he has to accept that serious setbacks can occur from time to time and the stock market can decline 80 to 90 percent. It can happen but in the long run, the Chinese economy will expand, as will the Indian economy.

The last 250 years have been favorable for the colonial powers of the Western World and Japan. They grew at the expense of the emerging economies. Now we're experiencing a reversal where the standard of living in the emerging world will grow, the balance of power is shifting to the emerging economies which in aggregate are larger than the G7. This transition will lead to huge geopolitical tensions and volatility.

John Nyaradi: Is there anything else you would like to add?

Dr. Marc Faber: The most serious issues I see are the increased involvement of the U.S.government in economic affairs and its war efforts in Iraq and Afghanistan, along with its money printing, to which I don't see an end. These unfunded future liabilities could mean we are headed to some kind of financial crisis in the next ten years. Social tensions will increase, and I'm afraid the U.S. could become more belligerent to distract attention from these problems and this could eventually lead to a major confrontation. All of this could be difficult to finance and lead to more money being printed and hyperinflation at the end of the day.

KEITH FITZ-GERALD

Keith Fitz-Gerald is Chief Investment Strategist of the Money Map Press LLC, as well as for *Money Morning*, a daily global investing news service with more than 500,000 daily readers in 30 countries. A former professional trader and licensed CTA advising institutions and qualified individuals, he is one of the world's leading experts on global investing, particularly when it comes to Asia's emergence as a global powerhouse.

He is a Fellow of the Kenos Circle, a think tank based in Vienna, Austria, that's dedicated to the identification of economic and financial trends using the science of complexity. Fitz-Gerald, his wife and two children split their time between the United States and Japan. Fitz-Gerald routinely travels the world in search of investment opportunities others don't yet see or understand. Keith is also the author of *Fiscal Hangover: Protect Your Money and Profit in the Global Economy*, published by John Wiley & Sons, November 2009.

John Nyaradi: Could you discuss your views of active management versus buy and hold?

Keith Fitz-Gerald: I have strong opinions on this subject. Buy and hold is more like "buy and hope." It's a marketing gimmick, not a management philosophy. If they blindly follow such things, millions will find themselves on the short end of the stick just like they did in 2000 and during the most recent crisis. The most successful investment approach, in my opinion, is buy and "manage." People can use any technique they want; voodoo bones, Pepsi bottles, whatever, as long as they have a method, they have studied it and understand it, and they work at it. That's why guys like Soros, Buffett, Rogers, Templeton, and others are the legends they are. In my opinion, consistent and disciplined active management is head and shoulders above buy and hold, particularly if the going gets rough like it has been lately.

John Nyaradi: Could you give us an overview of how you make your investment decisions?

Keith Fitz-Gerald: I'm a self-described techno-fundamentalist. I use a combination of technical and fundamentals to make investment decisions. The first step is to establish a broad-based global outlook that is scenario based and top down. I will develop three, four, five probable scenarios for the social, political and economic outlook for the next 12 to 60 months.

Once I do that, I drill down and figure the nuances as well as which sectors are likely to outperform under which specific conditions. Then I put together a playbook based on proprietary indicators and marry them to the scenarios. But it's a fluid system. The market is never the same and I don't believe any investor should be so set in his or her ways that he or she can't adapt. I'd rather plan for the certainty of returns rather than for the uncertainty of events.

John Nyaradi: You mentioned you use technical indicators. Which ones do you find to be most effective?

Keith Fitz-Gerald: Mine all incorporate nonlinear math and are probability centered and proprietary. The closest publicly known tools would be R Squared, Keltner Channels, or RSI, which together can be used to not only judge relative conditions under which investments may be at extremes, but also demonstrating the potential for reversals.

John Nyaradi: What's your view for the U.S. and global economy over the next three to five years?

Keith Fitz-Gerald: It's fairly clear that we're going to be hurting for a long time. It may take a while to come to terms with this but someday we're going to have to pay the piper. England fell into a decline that took decades to play out. The Pound was the reserve currency of the world and England didn't come back from the brink until they discovered oil in the North Sea. The United States was on top for 200 years and it could take a while for us to come back, especially if Bernanke & Co. continues on their present course of action (Dec. 2009) as they seem determined to do.

John Nyaradi: What macro trends/super sectors are we facing? How does this differ from prior crises?

Keith Fitz-Gerald: A super sector is a very interesting term because it gets to what I describe as globally unstoppable trends. I want to invest in high probability trades backed by billions, even trillions of dollars.

The unstoppable growth of China is clearly one that is a game changer. China is not just a player; it could be the greatest wealth creation in recorded history. Infrastructure is another with an estimated $40 trillion globally going into that sector in the next 30 years or sooner depending on which estimates you believe. Everyone needs electricity, rail, water, trucking. In terms of the crisis, what's different this time around is that we're also having a monetary revolution.

Money itself is a super sector and we're likely to see the complete revaluation of the global currency standard together with a near complete global recapitalization of global financial markets before this is done. The rise of the yuan and decline of the dollar will both be factors—perhaps even at the same time. And the unfortunate reality of the world we live in today is that war, terrorism, and ugliness are all growth businesses so I believe that companies that are defense oriented are going to be good bets.

John Nyaradi: What opportunities do you see for investors over the next three to five years?

Keith Fitz-Gerald: Follow the money. In contrast to what you hear on Wall Street, this isn't a terribly difficult proposition. The strongest economy on the planet is China and one of the weakest is the United

States. Anything tied to Asia, particularly China, should hold opportunity literally for decades to come. In the same vein, large multinational companies doing business in China, Brazil, India, and the Middle East could offer opportunities.

John Nyaradi: What traps and dangers do you see for investors over the next three to five years?

Keith Fitz-Gerald: Three dangers. The first is the failure to grasp the new reality of how money moves around the world and then getting left behind because they don't know how to participate. The average guy has a mere 6% international exposure in his portfolio and my data suggests it should be closer to 40–50% which would be a landslide change in attitude, not to mention invested assets.

The other things we're likely to see are huge periods of volatility and very violent movements in the markets. Psychologically speaking, this will be a very damaging decade and many people won't be able to handle it. The third risk is the failure to understand relationships between asset classes. We're closer to the beginning of a massive commodity bull run than the end, even though we've already had one heck of a run. This means that we could be in store for 6 to 10 years of declining equity values before things truly turn around.

John Nyaradi: A moment ago, you mentioned Asia and China, in particular. Could you discuss your outlook for China and Asia over the next three to five, even ten years?

Keith Fitz-Gerald: Sure. The only thing people need to understand is that the dragon is coming to lunch on Thursday. And the only decision you have to make is whether you want to be at the table or on the menu. China is a country of 1.3 billion people who save 35 percent of their income on average, a country flush with capital and that has a government completely committed to the success of their economic structure. What's more, they've saved up some $2.3 trillion dollars and now they're spending it. As Former Prime Minister Lee Kuan Yew of Singapore said succinctly, "China is not just another player ... it is the biggest player in the history of mankind." There will obviously be fits and starts, but overall the trend is higher, far higher.

John Nyaradi: What investment vehicles are your personal choices? ETFs, stocks, mutual funds, commodities, and why?

Keith Fitz-Gerald: I'm opportunity driven. I don't care what the vehicle is as long as it fills my requirement for certainty of returns. I dislike the fees associated with mutual funds; I think mutual funds are becoming obsolete.

John Nyaradi: What is your outlook for the price of gold, silver, oil over the next three to five, ten years?

Keith Fitz-Gerald: I'm generally bullish. It won't be a straight line but gold could be $2,000 within ten years. $2,500 is not out of the question, not because of inflation but because of a real move in the international banking community towards a hard asset global currency. On our present course, it's not improbable that the dollar could lose 50 percent of its value in the next five to ten years if we don't make changes. Washington believes the dollar is a weapon; what they don't understand is that the rest of the world thinks the dollar is a liability. Investors can play that; the dollar is a super sector.

John Nyaradi: Is there anything else you'd like to add?

Keith Fitz-Gerald: Yes. I look at markets today, and having studied history extensively, I'm very excited by what I see for one simple reason—the greatest upheavals inevitably lead to the greatest profits. Personally this feels bad, unemployment and recession and economic crises, but professionally I'm more excited than at any point in my career.

If you can separate the two and put in a buy and manage approach to the super sectors we've been discussing, the odds are you're going to do very well over the next ten to twenty years. This is the dawning of a new era of wealth, and the social upheaval we're witnessing right now is the key fundamental indicator that has proceeded every other golden age of wealth in history. I find that compelling.

TODD HARRISON

Todd Harrison is founder and CEO of Minyanville.com, a leading financial web site, and has 19 years of experience on Wall Street. He was a Vice President at Morgan Stanley and managing director of derivatives at The Galleon Group before joining $400 million hedge fund Cramer, Berkowitz as a partner, head of trading, and President from January 2001 to 2003. Todd has appeared on The FOX Network, CNBC, CNN, and Bloomberg as well as in financial magazines like *Business Week, Fortune, Barron's* and *The Wall Street Journal*. He also received an Emmy Award from The National Academy of Television Arts and Sciences for his role as Executive Producer of *Minyanville's World in Review*, the first and only animated business news show.

John Nyaradi: Could you discuss your views of active management versus buy and hold?

Todd Harrison: Having just emerged from the worst ten year stretch in stock market history, we heard a lot about how buy and hold was dead; I thought that proclamation was misplaced and reactive. By definition, a longer-term strategy is more viable following a massive equity decline and the odds of success incrementally decrease as the market climbs higher. In short, and entirely intuitive, the success of that strategy is determined by the time and price of entry.

John Nyaradi: Could you give us an overview of how you make your investment decisions? Technical indicators? Fundamentals? Both?

Todd Harrison: I have two buckets of capital, a long-term nest egg and an active trading account. With regards to the trading account, I look at the market through the lens of four primary metrics: fundamentals, technical, structural, and psychological. When viewed in isolation, each of those approaches has inherent flaws. Fundamentals are best at the top and worst near a low. Technical indicators often trigger buy signals higher and sell signals lower, after a stock has broken down. Structural factors—credit markets, derivatives, currency effects—can self-sustain in a cumulative manner until such time they overwhelm the system. Psychology, such as herding behavior, social mood, and risk appetites, often gain momentum until they snap. I've found, however, that if you properly assimilate those four metrics and align those ducks—something I call the "quack count"—the odds of an advantageous risk-reward greatly increase.

John Nyaradi: What's your view for the U.S. and global economy over the next three years? Five years? Ten years? What macro economic trends are we facing?

Todd Harrison: To appreciate where we are and where we're going, we must first understand how we got here. Coming out of the tech bubble, we were never allowed to take the medicine that would ultimately lay the groundwork for a sustained recovery. Instead, we were given fiscal and monetary drugs that masked the symptoms. The word "recession" became anathema when it's a natural progression of the business cycle and necessary for future growth. There is a huge difference between a legitimate economic recovery and debt-induced growth. Massive credit creation shifted risk but didn't eliminate it. In fact, the imbalances were *cumulative* and bubbled from technology to real estate to China to crude and finally, into the debt bubble, which I thought was the mother of all bubbles. But I was wrong; central banks around the world came to the rescue and created an echo bubble, or government.com. Peter Atwater offered an apt and somewhat scary analogy on Minyanville: If sovereign lifeguards saved corporate America, who will be left to save the lifeguards?

We inhaled an amazing amount of toxic debt that is tied together with a complex web of derivatives, the net result of years of unregulated financial engineering. How that evolves and manifests will set the stage for the next few years. There are a multitude of other potential pitfalls as well; pension shortfalls, state budgets, municipalities, sovereign debt, and what we at Minyanville call the "European Disunion." What if Greece is Bear Sterns, Portugal is Fannie Mae and Spain is AIG? We've pushed risk out on the time continuum but it hasn't disappeared, it simply changed shape.

This could play out in one of two ways: We can allow for debt destruction and deflation that will pave the way for true globalization. Much like everything they said about the Internet would be proved true—but not without a technology crash. The same can be said for globalization, in my view, but not without debt destruction. The other path is consistent with what we're currently doing, transferring risk from one perception to another, effectively giving the drunk another drink with the hopes they don't sober up. If we continue on this path, we could face the tricky trifecta of social acrimony, social unrest, and geopolitical conflict. World wars were born from economic hardship; that's an unfortunate and unavoidable truth.

John Nyaradi: What opportunities for investors/traders do you see over the next three, five, and ten years?

Todd Harrison: I see profound opportunities for those who can preserve capital, reduce debt, and remain financially aware and unemotionally attached. Proactive patience will be a virtue in what promises to be a reactive—and often scary—world. Surround yourself with people you trust who have skill sets that complement your own. If you can squirrel away some dry powder, there should be opportunities to pick up dollars for dimes in a multitude of situations.

John Nyaradi: What traps and dangers do you see for investors/traders over the next three, five, and ten years?

Todd Harrison: I touched on a few earlier—the state of the states, commercial real estate, pension shortfalls, and European "Disunion." Perhaps more concerning, however, are the unintended consequences of global policies. Social mood and risk appetites shape financial markets. One of the biggest misperceptions in financial market history is that the Crash caused The Great Depression when The Great Depression actually caused the crash. I don't share this to be an alarmist; I do so with hopes of increasing awareness of the cumulative nature of our current course.

John Nyaradi: What sectors do you see holding the most potential for gains over the next 1 to 3 years, sectors that could be super sectors and so outperform the general indexes?

Todd Harrison: Commodities should outperform in a normalized market; things we need to feed, power, and educate the world, in general, as well as rare earth elements, will always have an underlying bid. I would caution that should the deflationary scenario unfold, gains could be relative rather than absolute for a few years.

John Nyaradi: Anything else you'd like to add that's important to you or of which retail investors should be aware?

Todd Harrison: My grandfather, Ruby Peck, taught me two life lessons that are critical for future generations. All you have is your name and your word, and honesty, trust, and respect are the foundation construct for any successful endeavor.

GENE INGER

Gene Inger began his career at a major Wall Street firm, and he anchored KWHY-TV in Los Angeles, the nation's first financial television station, and later began portfolio management. His West & East Coast *Stock Market Today* shows later became FNN affiliates, which merged into CNBC (where he remains an original Market Maven).

Now retired from portfolio management, Gene publishes "The Inger Letter," IngerLetter.com, in which he assesses the day's events and comments on any unusual moves in the stock, bond, dollar, oil, and gold markets, with a particular emphasis on technology issues in computers & telecommunications.

John Nyaradi: Could you discuss your views of active management versus buy and hold?

Gene Inger: I believe in active management for the portion of assets in a portfolio that are not long term. I would never have 100 percent of funds in an active account.

John Nyaradi: Could you give us an overview of what your trading systems are based on, how they work?

Gene Inger: I use a combination of technical and a lot of psychology and monetary considerations. We're not in normal times and an understanding of the psychology of the present economic environment and what's wrong with monetary policy is very important. This is going to be a new era and you can throw out every conventional approach to valuation you've had for the last ten to fifteen years.

John Nyaradi: What's your view for the U.S. and global economy over the next three to five years? What macroeconomic trends are we facing?

Gene Inger: Slow growth at best. Double-dip recession at worst. How can you justify trusting the higher end of the P/E ratio and the same metrics as we've had in the past decade? We need to turn the clock back to the prior generation. We've had an epic debacle and I don't believe you recover particularly quickly from that. I don't believe the market has absorbed the price to be paid for profligacy, greed, unbridled consumer spending. How do you emerge from that overnight? I'm not a super bear. Prosperity may be in 2020 or 2030. The low may be behind us.

John Nyaradi: What opportunities for investors/traders do you see over the next three, five, ten years?

Gene Inger: I do see America coming back. Oil might be the next gold. I'm a great believer in reversion to the mean. I see opportunities in technology, particularly broadband.

John Nyaradi: What traps and dangers do you see for investors/traders over the next three, five, ten years?

Gene Inger: Dangerous traps are following crowd psychology and parabolic markets in either direction, playing a trend that's long been played. Once the music stops, the keyhole exit can be pretty slim.

John Nyaradi: What ETFs and sectors do you see having the potential to outperform the major indexes going forward over the next three, five, ten years?

Gene Inger: Gold but it most likely will be more volatile and sensitive. Oil will be pertinent for years to come. Alternative energies are more risky than oil because of political and technological changes.

John Nyaradi: Is there anything else you'd like to add?

Gene Inger: Avoid asset price bubbles, don't fight the last war. The rules of preceding post-war monetary policy will not be sufficient if we don't develop a strong manufacturing basis and trade policies that protect American businesses. We live in a multinational world but we're not going to solve domestic issues without domestic growth and domestic jobs. The current path is a prescription for something other than a new golden age.

CARL LARRY

Carl Larry is President of *Oil Outlooks and Opinions,* a newsletter offering daily insight and analysis into the oil markets. Carl has been writing commentary since 1990 and over the last ten years has focused exclusively on oil and the oil markets. He has presented his views from APPEC in Singapore to OPEC in Vienna and has been featured on Bloomberg Television, *The Wall Street Journal, New York Times,* AP and Reuters along with the "CBS Evening News with Dan Rather," CNBC and PBS.

John Nyaradi: Carl, what are the macro issues in the energy markets?

Carl Larry: In the big picture, energy is like death and taxes, its need is going to grow and we continue digging into a finite resource.

John Nyaradi: Could you talk about global supply and demand projections?

Carl Larry: The Far East, not just China, is growing rapidly; countries like Korea, India, Vietnam, and Singapore are going to put additional demand on energy resources, along with moderate growth in the United States. On the supply side, things right now depend upon political stability in places like the Middle East and Russia. Real supply is in decline in Mexico and is forecast for the North Sea as early as 2012. Mexico is in decline and they're our second main supplier behind Canada. Canada has vast supplies of oil but it's hard to get to in the form of oil sands and with environmental issues, heavy use of water and cost of production.

John Nyaradi: What about oil prices looking out over the next few years?

Carl Larry: It is fairly priced now and will increase with demand and be relative to incremental growth. A slight change to the upside in demand throws everything to the upside.

John Nyaradi: Will green energy by a factor?

Carl Larry: Green energy will be a factor 20 to 30 years down the road. Solar, wind, and hydro technology are getting better but the easiest way to produce energy is carbon based.

John Nyaradi: How does natural gas play into the global energy situation?

Carl Larry: If there was a way to stabilize natural gas for everyday use, we could reduce foreign oil consumption by 20 to 30 percent. The problem is the technology. It's an expensive, unstable product and it's hard to transport to places like China where it could cut their costs by 40 percent.

TIMOTHY LUTTS

Timothy Lutts is President and Chief Investment Strategist of Cabot Heritage Corporation, a widely respected publisher of investment newsletters since 1970. Cabot publishes eight newsletters which have been honored numerous times for being among the top investment advisories by *Timer Digest* and the *Hulbert Financial Digest* and he is also editor of *The Cabot Stock of the Month Report*.

John Nyaradi: Could you discuss your views of active management versus buy and hold?

Timothy Lutts: Buy and hold is fine for the masses, who are either unable or unwilling to devote the time and mental concentration required to observe the market's actions and commit to a sensible course of action. But for all the rest, and I assume that means the people reading this book, active management wins, hands-down, for several reasons.

Properly practiced, active management brings greater returns, and this is regardless of whether you choose to follow a value discipline, a growth discipline, or a momentum discipline. The rewards are there for the devoted investor. The hardest part of the business for most people is that they fail to learn from others' mistakes. All the mistakes have been made before, and you can read about them in all the classic books. But most people don't read the books. They jump right in—with insufficient knowledge—and they learn the hard way, by making their own mistakes.

The goal of the beginner should be to make as few big mistakes as possible. He should always be aware of the risk inherent in each trade. He should always have an exit plan. And he should keep records of his trades, both winners and losers, and review them periodicaly to see where he can improve.

John Nyaradi: Could you give us an overview of what your trading systems are based on, how they work?

Timothy Lutts: I'm a growth investor at heart, because my father, who taught me the business, is a growth investor. That means I like companies that are growing, and that have the potential to multiply manyfold from here. (Today, for example, that includes solar power companies, wind power companies, cutting-edge communications companies, Internet commerce companies in developing economies, and companies in a multitude of industries in China—both industrial and consumer-oriented.)

But I never buy a growth company unless the chart tells me other investors are thinking the same way. The best company on earth is a horrible investment if no one is buying the stock. So I watch charts carefully, looking for strength, increasing volume, supportive bases, breakouts, etc. Ideally, I want to get on after the stock has begun its ascent, but before the whales (whose billions will push it higher) get on board.

Finally, and perhaps most important, I pay careful attention to market timing, investing aggressively when the market is supportive and holding lots of cash when the market is in a destructive mood. One of my favorite aspects of the market is the psychological aspect of market timing. It took me a very long time to learn it, but it's proven so very valuable in recent years. It's simply this: When nobody wants to buy, when investors are throwing away stocks regardless of value, and when the future appears dim indeed (remember the fall of 2008), it's probably time to buy.

Contrarily, when the majority of investors are bullish (back in 2000, both my lawn guy and my barber were talking about investing), it's probably time to turn bearish. These cycles exist because of human nature, and I believe they always will, regardless of what technologies we use to trade, and regardless of what the companies we invest in actually do. So learning to recognize them and take advantage of them is critical. As a lifelong contrarian (my eighth grade teacher called me an iconoclast), finding investment success by going against the prevailing sentiment brings great satisfaction.

John Nyaradi: What technical indicators do you use and which ones do you find to be most effective?

Timothy Lutts: For the market, I like simple moving average, combined with advance-decline lines and our Two-Second Indicator, which monitors the number of stocks hitting new lows on the NYSE. As for individual stocks, I cut my teeth on Relative Performance lines, drawing them by hand as a teenager. Today I also like the 50-day moving average, and, as previously mentioned, increasing volume, supportive bases, and breakouts.

John Nyaradi: What's your view for the U.S. and global economy over the next three years? Five years? Ten years? What macroeconomic trends are we facing?

Timothy Lutts: Next to my desk, over the fireplace mantel, is a carved wooden plaque that reads, "MARKETS ARE NEVER WRONG; OPINIONS ARE." It's a quote from Jesse L. Livermore, who wrote the classic *Reminiscences of a Stock Operator*.

Respecting that truism, my first answer is that what I think doesn't matter. I trust the charts more than my own thoughts. Nevertheless, since you asked, I'm optimistic about the long-term trends in China, which has cash, surplus human capital, a growing middle class, and momentum. The fact that its government is nominally Communist is fairly irrelevant; in fact, Paul Goodwin, the editor of *Cabot China & Emerging Markets Report*, recently wrote a column in which he concluded it was more properly termed an authoritarian oligarchy. Brazil is attractive too, and I have hopes that India will get its act together; a China/India alliance could be powerful!

I think the U.S. has too much debt, and that politicians (both Republicans and Democrats) are not addressing the problem . . . but people keep electing them. Also, I think that demographically, the United States is headed for a big shift toward saving; the consumer economy of recent decades is gone. While many people are worried about inflation, I think this psychological shift toward saving will restrain inflation.

So I'm not very bullish on the U.S. economy as a whole, but I fully believe that hundreds and thousands of great little companies will continue to be founded and come public and provide great investment opportunities. In particular, I think there are great opportunities in alternative energy, more efficient, less polluting transportation, health care intelligence, and communications technology.

John Nyaradi: What opportunities for investors/traders do you see over the next three, five, and ten years?

Timothy Lutts: I think the above covers it.

John Nyaradi: What traps and dangers do you see for investors/traders over the next three, five, and ten years?

Timothy Lutts: I think too many people will continue to needlessly fear a repeat of the collapse of 2008, as well as the development of the bubble that preceded it. The fact is, these bubbles and crashes develop only once in a lifetime; everybody affected by the latest one will make sure they're not part of the next one, so there won't be a next one until all of us are gone . . . or senile.

John Nyaradi: What ETFs and sectors do you see having the potential to outperform the major indexes going forward over the next three, five, and ten years?

Timothy Lutts: Today, my thoughts lean toward China, Brazil, and alternative energy, but as trends change my opinions will change, too.

John Nyaradi: What investment vehicles are your personal choices, ETFs, stocks, mutual funds, commodities, etc. and why?

Timothy Lutts: Stocks, stocks, stocks. Because they're what I learned, because they're what I watch, and because they're more fun.

TOM LYDON

Tom Lydon is President of Global Trends Investments, a registered investment advisory firm managing assets for high net worth investors. He is also Editor of ETF Trends, a web site with daily news and commentary about the fast changing trends in the Exchange Traded Funds (ETF) industry. He is author of *The ETF Trend Following Playbook* and co-author of *iMoney: Profitable Exchange Traded Fund Strategies for Every Investor*. Tom serves on the Board of Directors for U.S. Global Investors and Rydex Investments and on PIMCO's Advisory Board for Investment Advisors.

John Nyaradi: I'd like to discuss your views of active management versus buy and hold.

Tom Lydon: Buy and hold is a strategy that no longer works for the average investor. Too many investors hung on during the Great Recession, having long been taught that if they just rode the market's dips and valleys, they would ultimately prevail. For their persistence, they were rewarded with losses of 40 percent, 50 percent or more in their retirement accounts.

As a result, millions of investors have been forced to postpone retirement or forget it altogether. Today, investing requires more active participation. We're in a new climate, where the markets can have sudden and prolonged corrections that investors can't afford not to sit out, otherwise they'll lose not only money, but time.

John Nyaradi: Why have you chosen ETFs over individual stocks or mutual funds?

Tom Lydon: ETFs are a superior product for a number of reasons: They cost less than mutual funds, on average. There are no early redemption fees, nor are there hefty minimums. They're transparent—you always know what you own. They're less risky than single-stock picking. They trade all day on an exchange like a stock. ETFs give investors the flexibility, tax-efficiency, liquidity, and transparency that investors need and want these days.

John Nyaradi: In your book, *The ETF Trend Following Playbook: Profiting from Trends in Bull or Bear Markets with Exchange Traded Funds*, you talk about trend-following methods. Could you describe what methods you use and how you use those to make trading decisions?

Tom Lydon: My trend-following discipline involves using the 200-day moving average to determine where we invest. When a position is above the 200-day, we're in; when it drops below, we're out. This discipline has you taking positions in time to enjoy any potential long-term uptrend, and it helps put a cap on your losses.

    The discipline also allows investors to focus on what the market is doing instead of relying on emotional cues that can lead them astray. We also consider other things when choosing an ETF, including assets under management, trading volume and diversification among its holdings.

John Nyaradi: What technical indicators have you found to work, if any?

Tom Lydon: The 200-day moving average.

John Nyaradi: What's your view for the U.S. and global economy over the next five years? Ten years?

Tom Lydon: In the next five and ten years, the U.S. economy's percentage of the global market cap is going to continue to shrink. Right now, only one-third of the world's market cap resides in the United States.

    Our economy is going to continue to see tempered growth after the Great Recession as we make up lost ground in unemployment—growth should gather steam as Americans once again find jobs and start to spend again. Globally, we're going to see more decoupling. Already, we're seeing some economies shift their focus to internal consumption rather than an over-reliance on exports.

    Emerging markets, in particular, are going to drive global growth. Right now, they make up 50 percent of global GDP, and that's projected to grow. Emerging market populations are becoming increasingly middle class and investors need to start paying attention to them, if they aren't already.

John Nyaradi: What opportunities for investors/traders do you see over the next five, ten years?

Tom Lydon: Commodities are going to be an area to watch; the world's population is projected to swell to 9 billion by the year 2040. More mouths to feed, emerging economies that are becoming richer and demanding a more Western diet, and growing production of biofuels will strain the agriculture supply. Investors should also continue to find commodities, particularly gold, appealing as both an inflation hedge and a safe haven.

Climate change is another hot-button issue; while the United States is just gearing up to implement more green energy, such as solar and wind power, other nations, such as China, are already becoming major drivers of growth in this sector. As the United States gets on board with international efforts to combat global warming, this sector could present major opportunities in the next several years.

John Nyaradi: What traps do you see for investors/traders over the next five to ten years?

Tom Lydon: One trap investors should be wary of is bubbles—we tend to have short memories. Despite the dot-com collapse having occurred just years earlier, millions of Americans convinced themselves that "this time it's different" when housing prices began to run amok. Will the lessons of the housing bubble be a distant memory by 2015 or 2020, and will we be making the same mistakes with the next bubble that comes along? Or will we be wiser next time and recognize what's happening and take steps to protect ourselves? It's going to be interesting to watch. It's something I hope investors will remember.

The next bubble I foresee is fixed income—as the economy recovers, interest rates are going to go up and bond mutual funds and ETFs are going to get hit. Investors poured trillions of dollars into these funds, and many of them may not realize the negative impact rising interest rates could have. It could have a big impact.

John Nyaradi: What ETFs and sectors do you see having the potential to outperform the major indexes going forward over the next five to ten years?

Tom Lydon: Commodities have the potential to outperform, for the reasons stated above. The technology sector could also be a standout— the United States and other nations continue to innovate at a pace that's never been seen before.

John Nyaradi: What do you see coming along regarding ETFs, new products, new opportunities, developments?

Tom Lydon: I think we'll see more ETF education—as more investors buy them, providers are working hard to make sure that everyone understands their funds by publishing white papers and webinars.

There are also more ETF bloggers than ever. More emerging market ETFs. Look for more single countries and sectors being offered. Look for emerging market asset class funds. Emerging market sector funds are also starting to catch on. More leveraged and inverse ETFs.

These funds have been enormously popular with investors since they launched. In bear markets, bear funds help investors hedge losses. In bull markets, they help investors maximize gains.

We could see more socially conscious funds. Many investors don't want to invest in companies that they view as unethical or environmentally destructive. There are also investors who want to invest in funds that align with their own religious beliefs, be it in Shariah-compliant ETFs or ETFs based on the Baptist or Catholic faiths.

JOHN MAULDIN

John Mauldin is a multiple *New York Times* Best Selling author and recognized financial expert. He has been heard on CNBC, Bloomberg and many radio shows across the country. He is the editor of the highly acclaimed, free weekly economic and investment e-letter, "Thoughts from the Frontline," that goes to over 1.5 million subscribers each week (you can subscribe at www.2000wave.com). His newest book is *The End Game*.

John Nyaradi: What's your view for the U.S. and global economy over the next three years? Five years? Ten years? What macroeconomic trends are we facing?

John Mauldin: The real issues are political and depend upon how we handle the large government deficit we're facing. Not only the United States but Japan and much of Europe, as well. We have to reduce those fiscal deficits because they're going to have a large negative effect on the economy. I can see a double dip recession because of coming tax hikes that will have an enormous negative effect on the US economy. From there, I see slow growth. It's going to take time; we've dug ourselves a deep hole. We are not in a classic business cycle recession but a deleveraging, balance sheet recession that's going to take five or six years to work through.

John Nyaradi: What opportunities for investors/traders do you see over the next three, five, ten years?

John Mauldin: It depends who you are. If you're capable of buying distressed real estate, there are some good opportunities there. I would stay away from index funds of all types because a continuing bear market is a real possibility. I'm starting to buy biotech stocks because I think that's going to become a bubble over the next decade. Every quarter I'm going to buy biotech stocks and build a portfolio over the next three or four years. At the bottom of the next recession which

I think will be in 2011, there will be more opportunities in emerging markets than developed markets. I would prefer to use active managers rather than buy stocks or ETFs on my own so someone is paying attention for me. I see opportunity in commodity and actively traded funds like one I'm associated with, CMGTX.

John Nyaradi: What traps and dangers do you see for investors/traders over the next three, five, ten years?

John Mauldin: We all have to watch and make sure the government doesn't continue to run deficits. If we don't get those under control we (the U.S.) could end up looking like Greece. If that happens, you want to own a lot of gold. I'm hopeful that we will display some common sense and deal with the deficit. If that doesn't happen, we'll have major problems. This deficit contagion could happen and come from anywhere around the world, Europe, Japan could be the next Greece, the world is very interconnected.

John Nyaradi: What sectors do you see holding the most potential for gains over the next one to three years, sectors that could be "super sectors" and outperform the general indexes?

John Mauldin: Commodities and gold. Biotech. Long and short commodity funds. In time, emerging markets will outperform the developed economies.

John Nyaradi: Anything else you'd like to add that's important to you. What would you tell someone just starting out?

John Mauldin: Get as broad an education as you possibly can. The world will change much faster than you can imagine. What you're prepared for today isn't what you're going to be doing in a few years. Patience is a position. You don't have to make it all at once. Be careful.

LAWRENCE G. MCMILLAN

Larry McMillan has authored two best-selling books on Options, including *Options As a Strategic Investment*, recognized as an essential resource for any serious option trader's library.

As president of McMillan Analysis Corporation, he authors the "Daily Volume Alerts," and edits and publishes "The Option Strategist," a derivative products newsletter covering equity, index, and futures options.

Recognized as an options trading industry expert, serious investors have relied on his insights, observations and recommendations for years and he is widely quoted in financial publications including the *Wall Street Journal, Futures Magazine, TheStreet.com* and *Barron's.*

John Nyaradi: Could you discuss your views of active management versus buy and hold?

Lawrence McMillan: Simply stated, there is never a reason to buy and hold. All positions should have some sort of stop loss and that criterion alone prevents the buy and hold strategy. There is no reason to hold stocks during long market downturns. So, using some sort of moving average as a trailing stop loss is advisable, in my opinion.

John Nyaradi: Could you give us an overview of how you make your investment decisions?

Lawrence McMillan: We are option traders, and we look for theoretical advantages in the implied volatility of the options. That drives not only the strategy we use, but which underlying stock we use, and which options on that underlying. We manage money for different types of clients (all in option-oriented strategies), and not all strategies are suitable for all clients. In the cases where we are looking for pure speculation—such as an outright long or short position, *not* dependent on option implied volatilities—then we use technical analysis to drive those decisions.

John Nyaradi: Do you use technical indicators and which ones do you find to be most effective?

Lawrence McMillan: Our broad market predictions use four basic technical indicators: the chart of the S&P 500 Index (SPX), equity-only put-call ratio charts (a sentiment indicator), market breadth (advances minus declines), and volatility—typically as measured by the CBOE's Volatility Index (VIX).

For individual stocks, we look at put-call ratios, composite option implied volatility, and option volume (heavy-option trading often shows where "insiders" are operating).

Once in a speculative position, we use a trailing moving average—typically the Chandelier Stop or perhaps just the simple 20-day moving average—as a way to let profits run while cutting losses.

John Nyaradi: What's your view for the U.S. and global economy over the next three years? Five years? What macroeconomic trends are we facing?

Lawrence McMillan: We have a strong, specific view on this. There has been and still is (as of February, 2010) a very strong correlation between the 1938–1939 stock market (as measured by the Dow) and the 2009–2010 stock market (as measured by SPX).

There are also strong economic, fundamental comparisons between the two time periods. Let's discuss those first, and then return to the stock market comparisons. In 1937, the economy went into a steep dive—a dive so steep that is would have actually been classified as another depression, but the word "recession" was invented at the time to describe what has happening. President Roosevelt had not previously been a pure Keynesian, but with the 1937 recession, he became one. Under Keynes' influence, the money spigots were opened and the old-time equivalent of TARP took place, flooding money into the economy. This is, of course, very similar to what happened in 2008.

Now back to the stock market. The Dow declined into a March bottom in 1938 and then rallied 58 percent into late 1938. In 2009, a similar decline into March marked the bottom of the market, and a 72 percent gain unfolded over the rest of the year. Both of these were liquidity-driven rallies, fueled by the Keynesian monetary policies of the Federal Reserve/Government. Statistically, there is an 89 percent correlation between the 1938 and the 2009 market movements. That is very high.

The actual high for the 1938 rally was in November, the day after Election Day, as the Republicans made significant gains in the House. It turned out that those November 1938 highs were not reached again until *seven years later!* However, the rally held together and was very near its highs as the calendar turned to 1939. But then problems began to develop, and there was a 10 percent market decline in January 1939 and by April, prices were 20 percent off their peaks.

A subsequent rally couldn't recover all those losses, though, and a bear market was under way that finally bottomed in 1942 at lower lows that those of March1938. From there, a bull market began, but—as just stated above—it took until 1945 to get back to the 1938 highs.

We expect something very similar to happen now, for the 1938–1945 time period is not the only one in history where it has taken the market six or seven years to recover after a severe financial dislocation. We do not necessarily think the market will trade below the March 2009 lows, but there will be a slow, grinding bear market for the next three years or so, and then a mediocre recovery. It will likely be 2015 or 2016 before the end-of-the-year 2009 prices are exceeded. And that will still leave SPX a long way below its 2007 all-time highs.

John Nyaradi: What opportunities for investors/traders do you see over the next three to five years?

Lawrence McMillan: Volatility will likely remain relatively high, so strategies involving hedge option selling will theoretically be viable. This would include covered call writing, for example.

Also, when volatility is high, short-term speculators can do well, provided they respect the volatility.

John Nyaradi: What traps and dangers do you see for investors/traders over the next three to five years?

Lawrence McMillan: Complacency will likely be a danger. In a slow, grinding bear market, it is easy to get lulled into doing nothing. Besides, many investors survived the last two bear markets by doing nothing, so they think they can do that again. They may not have fully recovered, but the 2003–2007 rally mostly made up for the 2000–2002 Bear Market, and the huge liquidity-driven rally of 2009 went a long ways toward soothing the wounds of the 2007–2008 Bear Market. We feel this will be a dangerous attitude to have in 2010 and the next few years.

John Nyaradi: You're a widely recognized expert in options trading. What types of option trades have you found to have the highest probability of success?

Lawrence McMillan: The simplest answer to that question is "Those with a high expected return." Expected return is a statistical calculation that evaluates the probabilities of a strategy or trade making money. It is not really applicable to outright holdings of long/ short stock or options, but rather to two- (or more) sided strategies, which could range from simple covered call writing, to complex ratio, or diagonal spreads. These are generally neutral strategies, for the most part, in which the option trader is not trying to predict stock price movement as much as he is trying to create a range of prices in which the strategy would profit. The greatest difficulty in using expected return is that one must estimate volatility of the underlying during the life of the position. That can be very difficult, although it is usually somewhat *less* difficult than trying to predict stock prices *per se*.

John Nyaradi: Are ETFs suitable for option trading? If so, what's the most effective category; indexes, sectors, country, commodities?

Laurence McMillan: ETF's have dampened volatility, and that is not usually to the option trader's benefit. For example, covered call writers of ETF's don't receive much in the way of option premiums. On the other hand, option buyers (speculators) may find the cheapness of ETF options attractive, provided that the ETF itself can move fast enough to generate speculative profits. Of course, broad-based ETF's, such as

SPY or QQQQ are instrumental in option trading, offering great liquidity, and the same opportunities that could be found in the more expensive SPX or NDX markets and options.

PAUL MERRIMAN

Paul Merriman is founder of Merriman, a registered investment advisory firm headquartered in Seattle, Washington, and he is editor of FundAdvice. com, a newsletter dedicated to investing in no-load mutual funds. Paul co-hosts "Sound Investing," a weekly radio broadcast named in 2008 as the "Best Money Podcast" according to *Money Magazine* and his newest book, *Live it up without Outliving Your Money: Getting the Most from Your Investments in Retirement*, published by John Wiley & Sons, has been revised and updated. He is also the author of *Investing for a Lifetime* and *Market Timing with No-Load Mutual Funds*.

Paul has been widely quoted in many national publications including *Money Magazine, U.S. News and World Report, Kiplinger's Personal Finance, USA Today, Barron's, Business Week, The Wall Street Journal, Investor's Business Daily*, and *Forbes* and has appeared on national television shows including "Wall Street Week" with Louis Rukeyser, PBS' "Nightly Business News" with Paul Kangas, plus many financial talk shows on CBS, CNBC, and CNN.

John Nyaradi: Could you discuss your views of active management versus buy and hold?

Paul Merriman: I'm an advocate of both. If someone believes in buy and hold, I feel my job is to make them the best buy and holder using the proper balance of equity and fixed income funds to address their loss limits. Market timing is for investors who don't want to invest without an exit strategy. Adding timing to a portfolio gives many investors a peace of mind they cannot get with buy and hold. Because there is an exit strategy with timing I find investors are comfortable with more equities than similar risk-oriented, buy and hold investors. For a small group of our clients we combine asset allocation, timing, and leverage.

John Nyaradi: Could you give us an overview of what your trading systems are based on, how they work?

Paul Merriman: Our portfolios range from 100 percent fixed income to 100 percent equities in 10 percent increments. The choice of fixed income and equities depends on an investor's risk tolerance and desire for return—95 percent of the timing we do is trend following and all of our timing systems are mechanical. We don't use any predictive timing systems. So our portfolios are a combination of mechanical asset allocation and mechanical timing.

John Nyaradi: What's your view for the U.S. and global economy over the next three years? Five years? Ten years? What macroeconomic trends are we facing?

Paul Merriman: I am unfortunately one of those people who have always believed that there's a catastrophic event right around the corner. That's why I'm personally more comfortable with timing than buy and hold. The big concern I have is whether people will start spending money or will they go back to the saving rates of the 1980s? If saving becomes a priority I suspect we are in for a lackluster decade for the economy and the market.

John Nyaradi: What opportunities for investors/traders do you see over the next three, five, and ten years?

Paul Merriman: All of the past data implies value over growth and small cap over large cap. I believe that will be true in both the U.S. and international markets. Plus, the international asset classes give us a currency hedge against a falling U.S. dollar. Also, it is highly unlikely that bonds will do better than stocks, as they did in the last decade.

John Nyaradi: What traps and dangers do you see for investors/traders over the next three, five, and ten years?

Paul Merriman: It's easy to know what we should have done in the past. There is no risk in the past. We know which trading systems would have made the most money or which systems would have had the least risk. But as markets continue to become more efficient, the likelihood that systems will perform as well in the future as they have in the past declines. Investors who build complex systems based on the past are likely to be very disappointed.

John Nyaradi: What ETFs and sectors do you see having the potential to outperform the major indexes going forward over the next three, five, and ten years?

Paul Merriman: I'm a strong believer in sector rotation and asset class rotation. Our systems are all mechanical so whatever floats to the top dictates where our money goes. If I had to predict the big winners for the decade, I would select U.S. and international small cap value and emerging markets.

John Nyaradi: What investment vehicles are your personal choices: ETFs, stocks, mutual funds, commodities, etc. and why?

Paul Merriman: Illiquid markets are still better accessed with relatively passive mutual funds. We trade ETFs and mutual funds in timing accounts. ETFs in illiquid markets have not outperformed passively managed funds in buy and hold accounts but have performed well in timing accounts.

John Nyaradi: Is there anything else you'd like to add?

Paul Merriman: Whether you're a buy and holder or market timer, asset allocation is always the most important decision.

ROBERT PRECHTER

Robert Prechter has written 14 books on finance, beginning with *Elliott Wave Principle* in 1978, which predicted a 1920s-style stock market boom. His 2002 title, *Conquer the Crash*, predicted the current debt crisis. Prechter's primary interest is a new approach to social science, which he outlined in *Socionomics—the Science of History and Social Prediction* (1999–2003). In 2007, *The Journal of Behavioral Finance* published "The Financial/Economic Dichotomy: A Socionomic Perspective," a paper by Prechter and his colleague, Dr. Wayne Parker. Prechter has made presentations on his socionomic theory to the London School of Economics, Cambridge University, MIT, Georgia Tech, MIT, SUNY and academic conferences. Read more at www.robertprechter.com.

John Nyaradi: Could you discuss your views of active management versus buy and hold?

Robert Prechter: Buy and hold in the very long run is a road to bankruptcy. Most corporate enterprises fail eventually. But buy and hold works at major bottoms. In October 1982, I wrote in *The Elliott Wave Theorist*, "This should be the first buy-and-hold market since the 1960s." (You can read about it in the Appendix to *Elliott Wave Principle*.) But this was a *timed* buy and hold.

The main problem with the idea of buy and hold is that it typically becomes popular late in bull markets. A small book published in 1917 called *One-Way Pockets* detailed how clients of brokerage firms typically trade in and out early in bull markets and become buy and holders near the top, so they ride the bear market all the way to the bottom.

There really is no such thing as non-active management. Everyone buys and sells; they just usually do it for bad reasons. But you need a method for figuring out what you should own. Most buy and hold advocates have none.

Most active managers are stock pickers. They give no thought to market timing. This is fine, as long as the market is rising. But when it falls, they are often caught in high-beta stocks that do worse than the averages. We saw it happen in 2008, when most of the best money managers of the bull market lost more than the S&P did.

I am in favor of any approach that improves returns in both bull and bear markets. Those who pick stocks, groups, or sectors should also attempt to discern better times to be long, short, or out.

John Nyaradi: Could you give us an overview of Elliott Wave Theory, what it's based on, how it works?

Robert Prechter: R. N. Elliott observed in the 1930s that the stock averages tend to move in a series of five waves when going in the same direction as the one larger trend and in a series of three waves when going against it. Smaller waves are components of larger ones, creating a patterned fractal. If you want to know more about this model of financial price behavior, check out *Elliott Wave Principle*.

John Nyaradi: In your book, the second edition of *Conquer the Crash*, you say, "The same authorities who said 'the worst can't happen' now claim that 'the worst is over.'" Could you describe the book's premises and themes?

Robert Prechter: *Conquer the Crash* predicted a very rare event: a collapse in the credit supply—which is deflation—and an ensuing depression. The events of 2008 were the opening act of these events. I expect this period to last at least until 2016. The book has four major sections. The first section lays out the case for a major, long-term top in stock prices and the economy. The second section explains what deflation is and why the Fed cannot prevent it. The third section is a manual on how to get your finances safe so you can hold onto your money in this challenging environment. The fourth section offers a list of safe banks, insurance companies, and money funds and a list of recommended services. The new second edition also includes my published market analysis and deflation essays through 2007.

John Nyaradi: Do you use any other technical indicators other than the Elliott Wave Principle? If so, which ones?

Robert Prechter: I use an array of sentiment and momentum indicators. The most valuable momentum indicators are breadth, divergence, TRIN, and volume, in that order. I do not use any of the popular price oscillators or moving averages. Sentiment indicators are valuable and must be analyzed as a group. But to get the most out of indicators, you must use them in the context of the Elliott Wave model, because it's the only template that can tell you how extreme the indicators will get.

John Nyaradi: What's your view for the U.S. and global economy over the next five years? Ten years? What macroeconomic trends are we facing?

Robert Prechter: The U.S. economy began a depression in 2001. It was slow in developing until 2008, when it began accelerating. As the economy approaches bottom later in this decade, economists should finally classify it as being in a depression. By that time, economists should be able to identify it as a depression. Before it is over, thousands of banks will close, and most debt issuers will default. At the low, the unemployment rate should exceed that of 1933. The U.S. government's solvency will also come into question.

John Nyaradi: What opportunities for investors/traders do you see over the next five, ten years?

Robert Prechter: We are going to have one of the greatest buying opportunities of all time at the next major low. Until then, investors should be completely out of all investment markets—real estate, stocks, commodities, and corporate and municipal debt—and in the safest cash and cash equivalents, in the safest institutions. Traders should be able to make a lot of money being short. The main problem there is the question of whether the banking system will be intact enough to ensure that speculators get paid.

John Nyaradi: What traps and dangers do you see for investors/traders over the next five, ten years?

Robert Prechter: The biggest traps are (1) optimism, which has been pinned to the ceiling for 11 years aside from late 2008 and early 2009, and (2) believing that the monetary system and economy should behave as they did in the advancing wave from 1933 to 1999. The false idea that it is still "business as usual" is behind Congress's outlandish spending, which just makes the economy weaker.

John Nyaradi: What ETFs and sectors do you see having the potential to outperform the major indexes going forward over the next five or ten years?

Robert Prechter: The real estate and financial sectors were our main picks for falling further than everything else. They are working out well so far. My book specifically predicted a fall in Fannie Mae stock, which was at its all-time high at the time. That worked out. I think most REITs and bank stocks will go to between ten cents per share and zero. I think companies that provide basic foodstuffs will stay in business.

John Nyaradi: What investment vehicles are your personal choices: ETFs, stocks, mutual funds, commodities, etc. and why?

Robert Prechter: Futures make the most sense to me. They are liquid and open almost around the clock.

John Nyaradi: Is there anything else you'd like to add?

Robert Prechter: Yes. Theory is not just of incidental interest; it's crucial. My "socionomic" hypothesis is that waves of social mood regulate social actions. This is why the stock market—which reacts immediately to changes in aggregate optimism and pessimism—moves ahead of news. News is the report of events that were set in motion by changes in social mood that have already occurred. Sometimes the market reacts briefly to news, but this is an emotional reaction, which is transient. Within an hour or so the market is always where it should be with respect to social mood. But these continual, brief reactions convince people that news moves the market. This belief is why most investors lose money over a full cycle; they are always looking at a seriously lagging indicator. For more on this idea, you might want to read my books and papers on socionomics. It's a whole new way of looking at the world of finance. Visit www.RobertPrechter.com for links.

JIM ROGERS

Renowned investor Jim Rogers is cofounder of the Quantum Fund and creator of The Rogers International Commodity Index. He is the author of several books including, *A Bull in China: Investing Profitably in the World's Greatest Market, Hot Commodities*, and *A Gift to My Children: A Father's Lessons for Life and Investing*.

John Nyaradi: Jim, what sectors do you see as being the two or three super sectors over the next three to five years?

Jim Rogers: Commodities. Commodities are going to be the place to be. If the world's economy improves, there are going to be shortages. If it doesn't, printing so much money always leads to higher prices. So either way, commodities should be good. Also some foreign currencies.

John Nyaradi: What's your forecast for gold?

Jim Rogers: I expect gold to get to $2,000 during the course of this bull market and the bull market has years to go as far as I can see.

John Nyaradi: What about silver? What about oil?

Jim Rogers: Silver should do better on a percentage basis than gold, just because it's down so much from its historic highs. The surprise in oil is how high the price will go over the next decade. The world's known reserves are declining very steadily. We're all going to be very surprised during the next bull market.

John Nyaradi: What's your outlook for China?

Jim Rogers: I expect China to be the great country of the 21st century. They'll have more growth and plenty of setbacks but they'll rise to power and glory. Teach your children and grandchildren Chinese.

John Nyaradi: What do you see for the U.S. dollar?

Jim Rogers: The dollar is a terribly flawed currency. I expect it to lose its status as the world's reserve currency.

John Nyaradi: Can the United States get back on the right track? What will it take?

Jim Rogers: It's never too late to turn it around, but it will require a great deal of pain. It won't happen because no politician will get elected who will stand up and say we've made mistakes, we're going to have to do some things like slash spending, change education and health care. Once it starts hurting, people are going to say I don't like this pain, let's stop, let's do something else.

John Nyaradi: If you were a young man starting out today, what would you do?

Jim Rogers: If I were 22, I would learn Chinese. I would hope I was smart enough to have already learned Chinese, and I would go to Asia and get involved in natural resources in one way or other. There are many ways to do that.

MATTHEW SIMMONS

Matthew R. Simmons is Chairman Emeritus of Simmons & Company, the only independent investment bank specializing in the entire spectrum of the energy industry. Founded in 1974, the firm has acted as financial advisor in nearly $142 billion of transactions (as of 9/30/09), including 562 merger and acquisitions worth nearly $98 billion.

Mr. Simmons received a Masters Degree with distinction in Business Administration from Harvard Business School and founded Simmons & Company International. He serves on numerous boards including the Board of Deans Advisors of Harvard Business School and is a member of the National Petroleum Council, Council on Foreign Relations, and The Atlantic Council of the United States. In addition, he is a former Chairman of the National Ocean Industry Association. Mr. Simmons is a Trustee of the National Trust for Historic Preservation and the Farnsworth Art Museum in Maine. He is the author of *Twilight in the Desert: The Coming Oil Shock and the World Economy*.

John Nyaradi: Matthew, what are the macro issues in the energy markets?

Matthew Simmons: The conventional wisdom has been wrong for 40 years. Oil and gas is the single largest industry in the world, the next largest is power generation, the third is water. Energy was deemed to be a dead industry since the early 1950s and most institutions stayed away from owning energy stocks. But now oil and gas flows have peaked and are going into decline. The average age of a skilled oil services worker is 60 years old, the infrastructure is in decline, and if we don't go on the biggest spend ever, there will be an energy shock that could be the last crisis we'll ever have. If you don't understand energy, it's like being at the start of the Industrial Revolution and saying I don't want to invest in the Industrial Revolution.

John Nyaradi: Could you address global demand projections?

Matthew Simmons: Global demand for oil and energy is virtually impossible to stop. Just to keep the oil supply flat between now and 2030 will require four Saudi Arabias. Two more Saudi Arabias will be needed just to supply modest projected growth.

John Nyaradi: What about U.S. supply and demand?

Matthew Simmons: U.S. oil production peaked in 1970 and has been in slow decline ever since.

John Nyaradi: What are price projections like going out over the next five or ten years?

Matthew Simmons: Prices have to go way higher. Looking at the summer of 2009, $140 per barrel is not outrageously expensive; it's less than 24 cents a cup. There's no evidence that high prices will slow down demand. The issue isn't price but availability. Demand is insatiable and supply is waning. Useable oil always has to equal supply.

John Nyaradi: Could you talk about China and India and their forecasts for growth?

Matthew Simmons: The United States uses 25 barrels of oil per year per person. Europe uses 18–20, Mexico uses 6.5, China uses less than 2 and India uses less than 1. China has 20 cars per 1,000 people and we have 900 per 1,000 people. China is the largest purchaser of cars in the world. If China and India together get just as big as Mexico is, we would need an extra 45 million barrels of oil per day.

John Nyaradi: What about peak oil theory? When do we run out of oil?

Matthew Simmons: Never. That's the single most misunderstood aspect of the debate on peak oil. We're not running out of oil. The flow rate is peaking. The irreversible decline of flow rate around the world makes it virtually impossible to get back to maximum production. The era of sweet oil is gone. Oil is becoming heavier and sour. The Saudis are changing their marker from West Texas Intermediate to sour. Oil production will be more energy intensive, have lower flow, require more refining and use more water to get the same production.

John Nyaradi: Anything else you'd like to add?

Matthew Simmons: Liquid ammonia is the future. You create wind where it exists, on the water, use wind to create electricity and combine ocean water and electricity and then separate out liquid ammonia which can burn like gas but with no carbon. Maine will be Menlo Park, the Silicon Valley of energy.

SAM STOVALL

Sam Stovall is Chief Investment Strategist at Standard and Poor's Equity Research and is Chair of the S&P Investment Policy Committee. He is the author of *The Seven Rules of Wall Street: Crash-Tested Investment Strategies That Beat the MarketSector Investing*, and *Standard and Poor's Guide to Sector Investing*. He also writes a weekly report, *Stovall's Sector Watch*, in which he discusses sector momentum and history. He is a Certified Financial Planner, received an MBA in Finance from New York University and is widely quoted in the financial and business press.

John Nyaradi: Could you give us an overview of your trading methodology, how it works? How you make decisions and use sector rotation?

Sam Stovall: I am an emotional investor so I try to extract emotion and take a rules-based approach to investing. I tend to use momentum-based techniques. Regarding sector rotation, the market leads economic expansions by six to nine months and so you can look to sector rotation to get an idea of where we think the economy is headed. When we see all sectors above water and in positive territory that is typically a signal of the beginning of a bull market. History is a great guide but it's not gospel.

John Nyaradi: In your book, *The Seven Rules of Wall Street: Crash-Tested Investment Strategies That Beat the Market,* you mention seven rules upon which you could build a portfolio. One was "There's no free lunch." Could you discuss that?

Sam Stovall: The saying goes, "There's no free lunch on Wall Street." And I say, "Who says?" If you can get increased return with lower risk, that's a free lunch. I'm getting something for nothing and that's where low correlation among sectors kicks in, owning sectors where one zigs while the other zags. Since 1990, Technology has been the best performing sector, up +8.9 percent annually compared to +5.8 percent for the S&P 500, but with a substantially higher standard deviation and higher risk. The Consumer Staples sector has the lowest correlation with Technology, so if you went 50/50 percent with Technology and Consumer Staples, you would have gotten a +9.6 percent return with lower risk. That's what I call a free lunch. Of course, past performance is no guarantee of future results.

John Nyaradi: What's another of your favorite rules?

Sam Stovall: "Sell in May and walk away" but where should you walk to? The rule says that that historically the six best months of the year are November through April and so investors should be in the market during those months and in cash from May through October. But if you take a rotational approach and during the six months from May to October move to 50/50 percent Consumer Staples and Health Care and then in November through April, move 1/3 each to Financials, Industrials, and Materials, your returns would have gone from +5.8% to +12%. Of course, past performance is no guarantee of future results but that is what history shows us.

John Nyaradi: What's your view for the U.S. economy over the next three to five years? What macro trends are we facing?

Sam Stovall: We're talking in December 2009, and we seem to be coming out of recession. Expansions last about five years or so and so we think this one will last into 2013. At this point, it looks like growth is likely to be below trend but either of these outlooks could change anytime along the way.

John Nyaradi: What traps and dangers do you see for investors over the next three to five years?

Sam Stovall: I'm a novice coin collector and there's a saying that you should buy and read the book before you buy and sell the coin. In other words, know what you own or what you're going to own, but most of all know yourself. Investing is a journey and you must ask yourself, "Do I want to drive or have someone else do the driving?" and don't become too optimistic about your own abilities.

CLIFF WACHTEL

Cliff Wachtel is the Chief Market Analyst for AVAFX, a leading online trading site for global currency, commodity, and stock index trading. He has attended Vassar College (Cum Laude) and Cornell University's MBA program, and is a Certified Public Accountant. Cliff provides institutional daily and weekly analysis and recommendations on international forex, gold, oil, and equities markets. He is a leading financial market analyst on major financial web sites and is listed in the "Who's Who of Financial Bloggers."

John Nyaradi: Could you discuss your views of active management versus buy and hold?

Cliff Wachtel: Buy and hold is acceptable for income-oriented stock portfolios, those with an emphasis on steady income more than capital gains.

   If the goal is capital gains, then you've really little choice but to attempt active management. Few growth stocks have managed to deliver steady long-term returns, and even then, will they be up when/if you need to sell? Over the past 50 years, we were in an environment in which demographics provided a growing pool of young, risk-hungry investors that supported a long-term rising stock market. Changes in technology and the availability of cheap labor were slower. Just considering how communications technology brought competition from cheap foreign labor and the aging demographics in the developed world and its loss of economic dominance makes the thought of blindly holding almost any asset over decades look foolhardy.

John Nyaradi: Could you give us an overview of how you make your investment decisions?

Cliff Wachtel: I use a mixture of fundamental analysis and technical tools to get the big picture and an overall thesis or theme, as well as for determining entry and exit points, both targets and stop losses. That gives me an overall theme: growth and risk versus defensive and recessionary. That suggests what specific instruments to consider going long or short.

   Divergences between trends in forex, commodities, and stocks can be an incredible leading indicator for stocks, especially because they tend to be ignored by the masses and mass media. Forex and commodity markets often telegraph future moves in stocks via negative or positive divergences. Risk currencies (AUD, NZD, CAD, EUR) and commodities should be moving in the same direction as stocks. Safe haven currencies (JPY, USD, CHF) move in the opposite direction because they rise in times of fear, when risk assets are falling. Because they are more sensitive to international demand forces that ultimately hit U.S. stocks, forex and commodity markets often reverse before stocks.

John Nyaradi: Do you use technical indicators and which ones do you find to be most effective?

Cliff Wachtel: The ideal technical tool tells you what everyone else will be thinking, just before they think it, so you can get in early in the move. Put a slightly more cynical way, one of the chief values of technical tools lies in how widely they're followed, because then they do a better job of showing you what everyone else is thinking. My old standards include the most popular moving averages, Bollinger Band combinations, Fibonacci retracements, and trend and channel lines, any obvious price levels that present repeated support or resistance and popular chart patterns like double tops. As one who follows global forex and commodities as well as stocks for a living, I also like to watch for the above divergences for the above stated reasons. They're reliable and intermarket analysis is not widely followed.

John Nyaradi: What's your outlook for the U.S. dollar over the next three to five years?

Cliff Wachtel: All major currency groups have been expanding money supply, most have relatively aging populations and rising debt loads so it's very tough to gauge which is likely to be the best or the least ugly (same thing in forex), never mind how the markets will actually interpret things. Regarding the future of the dollar, I believe that the biggest economic issue for the U.S. and the dollar is how to resolve the problems stemming from the mountain of debt and money printing that is eroding the dollar's value. We have the likely threat of impending inflation, erosion of savings and thus an impoverished elderly population whose savings are essentially being stolen by economic policy makers.

But if the U.S. can grow better than most competing currency groups, the U.S. dollar should gain on the others, and vice versa. That's historically been the case for most currencies; they act like stock shares in an economy. Despite the current mood, I still think the U.S. has at least as good a chance to remain economically dominant as any other developed nation.

John Nyaradi: What's your outlook for gold over the next three to five years?

Cliff Wachtel: Mostly moving opposite the dollar, because it is a hedge against fiat currency. Also, again, forex is all relative, so the strongest currency need only be the least ugly, and that may be the dollar's great hope.

John Nyaradi: What's your view for the U.S. and global economy over the next three years? Five years? Ten years? What macroeconomic trends are we facing?

Cliff Wachtel: One of the biggest issues I see is demographics and it's one that will affect everything. America is barely keeping up at replacement level birthrates. Europe and Japan are in population decline.

This has many ramifications because the investing patterns and the needs of old versus young are very different. Demand for goods and services are very different. Demands placed on governments are very different. For example, older investors seek steady income while the young are more open to investing in higher risk and growth instruments. Furthermore, a shrinking pool of productive earners producing taxable wealth will have to carry the growing burden of a larger group of elderly consuming greater portions of that wealth.

Shifting demographics will offer opportunities for those who can best meet that new demand, provide things like cost-effective healthcare or housing solutions for the elderly, along with technologies that allow older workers to work longer or telecommute.

A second macro issue is the need to develop cheap energy. Even with subpar growth, more energy will be needed to sustain industrialization and growing populations, and we don't yet have any viable substitute for fossil fuels at their current prices. Fuel equal to $200/bbl means a step down in living standards, barring any massive technological fix that reduces our needs to the same degree. The modern world runs on cheap energy, and we're running out of it with the current technologies. Just imagine life with a perpetual power outage, or if you can only afford electricity for a few hours a day? Ditto for housing, transportation, food, and water.

John Nyaradi: What opportunities for investors/traders do you see over the next three, five, ten years?

Cliff Wachtel: Anything that provides those needs just discussed in a cost-effective way or that enables significant conservation of those declining resources.

John Nyaradi: What traps and dangers do you see for investors/traders over the next three, five, or ten years?

Cliff Wachtel: Preserving wealth as all currency groups debase the value of their fiat money, while maintaining enough liquidity. For Americans, clearly one of the biggest changes will be the need to deal with forex, if for no other reason than diversification of liquid assets, just like one would in stock sectors.

John Nyaradi: What investment vehicles are your personal choices, ETFs, stocks, mutual funds, commodities, etc. and why?

Cliff Wachtel: For short-term trading: actual forex pairs or commodities (or their corresponding CFDs or ETFs), because with proper risk management, the risk/reward ratio can be very good. For the longer term—because predicting market direction is so hard—I rarely invest in anything that isn't paying a steady income, be it a long-term held forex pair for carry-trade that earns interest or income stocks. I tend to avoid mutual funds just because I haven't seen good value in them.

Forex ETFs can also be a very good, simple, long term way to have currency diversity, simply because forex trends tend to be long lived. Forex trends are driven by interest rates, economic growth, geopolitics, capital, and trade flows and these don't change quickly so you don't have to notice an opportunity fast.

GABRIEL WISDOM AND MICHAEL MOORE

Gabriel Wisdom is Founder and Managing Director of American Money Management. He is also the President of AMM Funds, which includes two publicly traded, no-load mutual funds. He has over 25 years experience in the securities industry, hosts a daily talk show on the Business Talk Radio Network, and is the author of *Wisdom on Value Investing: How to Profit on Fallen Angels*, published by John Wiley and Sons.

Michael J. Moore is Chief Investment Officer of American Money Management. He provides research and analysis and oversees trading for institutional and individual portfolios. Mike earned his BS in Finance from Boston College, is a member of Mensa International, and is co-manager of the Fallen Angels Value & Income Funds.

John Nyaradi: Could you discuss your views of active management versus buy and hold?

Gabriel Wisdom and Michael Moore: We view the practice of buy and hold as a popular myth. Periodically, you might find an investment that compounds book value at a high rate of return (>15%), and as long as the company continues compounding at this rate, we would hold for the long-run to benefit from compounding rates of return. More often, buying and holding regardless of market conditions, increases your chances of encountering recessions, crashes, and company specific disappointments.

"Buy and hold" investing may work well for a very large shareholder, who is effectively a company insider. Similar to a small business owner, this kind of investor has the ability to affect change in an organization, and may even have the power to direct the company's resources to their benefit (special dividends, share buybacks, etc.).

Like most investors in public companies, however, we are outside passive minority investors (OPMI). Since we have no real say in how a company conducts its operations (other than limited proxy power), the only vote we're left with is whether to sell or buy more. Companies, like people, experience a fairly predictable life-cycle, in which there are growing pains, midlife crises, booms, and busts along the way. As active managers, we want to position ourselves in stocks that have the ability to generate high returns, at prices that make economic sense. Some we may buy and hold for a few months, others for several years. Like farmers who look forward to a bountiful harvest, we will end up selling our stocks at some point. This generally occurs when the security becomes overpriced, or a negative fundamental change occurs in the business, or we just need to raise cash in order to buy something better.

John Nyaradi: Could you give us an overview of how you make your investment decisions?

Gabriel Wisdom and Michael Moore: We look at three primary factors: Quality, Value, and Timing. Quality relates to the company's ability to generate a high return on shareholder equity. With thousands of publicly traded companies to choose from, there is no need for us to settle on low quality businesses (narrow profit margins, high debt load, etc.). Generally speaking, we want to own businesses that have rising revenue and can return more than 15 percent on shareholder equity, or there is good reason to believe that they will be able to do this going forward. Additionally, balance sheet strength is an important component as we don't want to invest in businesses that require significant debt financing to run operations.

It's been said, "There are no toxic investments, just toxic prices." Once we find an investment that meets our criteria for quality, we try to assess a reasonable price for the business. Excellent, high-quality stocks (or bonds) that trade at high prices still make for bad investments. For example, Qualcomm is an excellent, well-run company in our estimation, however at a split adjusted $100 a share in January of 2000, it was a horrible investment. Since then, the company's shares are down more than 60 percent, while their earnings have more than doubled in the same time frame.

The third area is timing. Everything runs in cycles, and as investors we need to assess what time of the market it is. Macroeconomic and geopolitical factors can affect asset prices in ways not always obvious to the casual observer. For us, trying to understand the stage of the business and economic cycle that we are operating in adds another layer of risk management to our process.

In addition to macro-oriented analysis, we also consider the technical condition of both the market and/or the company that we are considering for investment.

John Nyaradi: Do you use technical indicators and which ones do you find to be most effective?

Gabriel Wisdom and Michael Moore: Head and Shoulders patterns, Cup and Handle formations, Gaps, and Moving Averages are the four technical patterns/indicators that we find most useful.

John Nyaradi: What's your view for the U.S. and global economy over the next three years? Five years? Ten years? What macroeconomic trends are we facing?

Gabriel Wisdom and Michael Moore: As people get older, their priorities and spending habits change. The average 30-year old wants to borrow money to buy a house, a nice car, or whatever. At 60, objectives change and studies have shown what an aging population can do to an economy . . . like Japan. In the U.S. and many parts of Europe, someone is turning 60 every seven seconds. Mature populations increase the odds for stagnant, deflationary economies.

Over the next three years we expect a rocky road as the recovery transitions from an artificial, primarily stimulus driven recovery to one driven by the private sector. Market prices seem to be disconnected from economic reality at this point in the recovery, and may keep the Dow Jones Industrial Averages at or near 10,000 for a prolonged period.

It wouldn't surprise us to see a continuation of the economic recovery (with a speed bump or two along the way) coupled with a weakening equity market for a period of time. There are any number of macro-factors that could facilitate this process. Currently, sovereign debt default concerns are at the top of the worry list.

John Nyaradi: What opportunities for investors/traders do you see over the next three, five, and ten years?

Gabriel Wisdom and Michael Moore: Volatility, as measured by the VIX, hit all time highs just below 90 in 2008 providing an opportunity for short and intermediate-term traders to make money on both sides of the market. 2009 saw a steady decline in the VIX to end the year at just above 21. Unlike the post 2003 recession, where volatility steadily declined for three years, we would expect the next three plus years to see a return of elevated volatility as economic forces shift. Nimble traders should find ample opportunity in this kind of an environment.

John Nyaradi: What traps and dangers do you see for investors/traders over the next three, five, and ten years?

Gabriel Wisdom and Michael Moore: Investors should guard against becoming complacent *after* major market moves. The experience during the secular bull market of the 1980s and 1990s was one of a generally rising stock market.

In our view, we have been in a secular bear market since 2000. This bearish period has been marked by multiple mini-bull markets. Optimism rises once the mini-bull market is close to peaking, as investors recall the rising tide that drove markets higher from 1983 to 2000. Investors hanging on to this view that the market will trend higher over the next five to ten years may be in for a rude awakening. We think there's a reasonable chance that this secular bear is only half over. Still, this environment should provide ample opportunity for active investors to generate returns.

John Nyaradi: What investment vehicles are your personal choices, ETFs, stocks, mutual funds, commodities, etc., and why?

Gabriel Wisdom and Michael Moore: We prefer to invest in stocks and ETFs. They are simple and typically provide for ample liquidity, which is necessary if we want to remain nimble. ETFs tend to work better for us when we are playing particular market themes.

John Nyaradi: What sectors do you see holding the most potential for gains over the next one to three years, sectors that could be super sectors?

Gabriel Wisdom and Michael Moore: We believe that over the next three to five years the deflationary forces that have marked this period will ultimately give way to inflation. Resource related sectors like oil and gas, precious metals, and agricultural commodities should begin to benefit as this transition unfolds. It is important to note that most of these sectors are currently in poor technical condition (2010) and this transition may not begin in earnest for awhile. In the meantime, high quality, dividend-centric stocks look attractive relative to most other assets.

John Nyaradi: Anything else you'd like to add?

Gabriel Widsom and Michael Moore: Avoid "dogs," and buy the CATS (cheap and timely securities).

CONCLUSION

In this chapter we've had the privilege of listening to some of the best minds on the investment and economic landscape today and hear their insights and opinions regarding our economic futures, where we are, and where we might be going.

Clearly there are common themes among these experts but also very unique and interesting differences in approach, outlook, strategies, and tactics. Just like you or me, every investor sees the world through his or her own unique lens and interprets information in his or her own unique way.

The experts we've just listened to have particularly well-proven lenses through which they view the investing landscape ahead, and everyone, regardless of expertise or experience, can gain from what these experts have to say.

We've now come to the end of our discussion of super sectors and how to find them and trade them in an actively managed, tactical trading program. We've looked at simple trading systems that anyone could use to help protect themselves from bear markets and we've looked at more complex trading systems for people who want to get more involved in actively managing their money.

We've made an in-depth study of ETFs and why they're a superior product in today's environment and we've studied sector rotation principles and the psychology of trading. Finally, we've taken a close look at five sectors that could be super sectors going forward over the next three to five years and heard from experts about their views of what these super sectors might be.

All of these things should prove useful in navigating the challenging waters ahead. In my opinion, the rules of investing have changed and maybe changed forever. Because of the bear market and subsequent incredible level of government intervention and because of the mega trends we've discussed, we now find ourselves living in a different world.

In this different world, it's very likely that old rules and techniques won't be effective in the years ahead. Those who adapt will survive and prosper. Those who don't adapt will face an uncertain and dangerous future.

Finally, I invite you to visit www.SuperSectors.net for more valuable information about sector rotation using Exchange Traded Funds.

There you'll be able to subscribe to a special membership offer from *Wall Street Sector Selector*, my online newsletter covering sector rotation and Exchange Traded Funds, as well as get more in-depth research, reports, and links to other leading financial web sites and portals.

By taking advantage of as many resources as possible, you will increase your probability for success and I would urge you to educate and arm yourself with the tools you'll need to successfully face the challenges that will be coming in the difficult days ahead.

Thanks so much for spending your valuable time with me. It is my sincere hope that you will be one of the winners and that you'll be able to succeed at the challenging task of active, tactical trading, and that you'll find peace and joy and prosperity throughout all your coming years.

All the best,

JOHN NYARADI
Publisher
Wall Street Sector Selector

ETF Resources

WEB SITES

www.SuperSectors.net

SuperSectors.net is the dedicated web site for *Super Sectors: How To Outsmart the Market Using Sector Rotation and ETFs*.

At SuperSectors.net you'll be able to subscribe to a special membership offer from Wall Street Sector Selector, my online newsletter covering sector rotation and Exchange Traded Funds, as well as get more in-depth research, free reports, and links to other leading financial web sites and portals.

EXCHANGE TRADED FUNDS PROVIDERS

There are many Exchange Traded Fund providers and below is a partial list of major providers with which I am familiar. All ETF providers below and mentioned throughout this book are registered trademarks of the specific corporation and the author has no affiliation with any of the corporations mentioned and no recommendations as to suitability or performance is made or to be implied. This list is for informational purposes only.

iShares: www.ishares.com; U.S. equities, sectors, international, commodity and fixed income ETFs.

Market Vectors: www.vaneck.com; Exchange Traded Funds and Exchange Traded Notes including hard assets, currency, and international.

Merrill Lynch HOLDRS: www.holdrs.com; trust issued receipts in sectors, including Biotech, Broadband, Internet, and Wireless.

PowerShares; powershares.com; actively managed ETFs, sectors, U.S. equity, commodity, currency, international, fixed income.

ProShares: proshares.com; leveraged and inverse Exchange Traded Funds.

RydexSGI: rydex-sgi.com; leveraged, sector broad market, currency Exchange Traded Funds.

Select Sector SPDRs: sectorspdr.com; nine sector Exchange Traded Funds.

WisdomTree: wisdomtree.com; emerging markets, currency, small cap, non U.S. sector Exchange Traded Funds.

Direxionshares: direxionshares.com; leveraged Exchange Traded Funds, bull and bear, market cap, sector and fixed income.

BOOKS

Connors, Larry, Alvarez, Cesar, and Connor Research LLC. 2009. *High Probability ETF Trading: 7 Professional Strategies to Improve Your ETF Trading.* Jersey City, NJ: TradingMarkets.

Faber, Marc. 2008. *Tomorrow's Gold: Asia's Age of Discovery*, Hong Kong, Japan: CLSA Books.

Fitz-Gerald, Keith. 2009. *Fiscal Hangover: How to Profit From The New Global Economy* (Agora Series) Hoboken: John Wiley and Sons.

Lydon, Tom. *The ETF Trend Following Playbook: Profiting from Trends in Bull or Bear Markets with Exchange Traded Funds.* Upper Saddle River, NJ: FT Press.

Mauldin, John F., and Mauldin, Tiffani. 2010. *Eavesdropping on Millionaires: Secrets of the World's Wealthiest Investors.* Hoboken: John Wiley and Sons.

McMillan, Lawrence G. 2002. *Options As a Strategic Investment.* Upper Saddle River, NJ: Prentice Hall.

Merriman, Paul A. 2008. *Live It Up Without Outliving Your Money!: Getting the Most From Your Investments in Retirement* Hoboken: John Wiley and Sons.

Prechter, Robert R. 2009. *Conquer the Crash: You Can Survive and Prosper in a Deflationary Depression* Hoboken: John Wiley and Sons.

Rogers, Jim. 2009. *A Gift to My Children: A Father's Lessons for Life and Investing.* New York: Random House.

Simmons, Matthew R. 2006. *Twilight in the Desert: The Coming Saudi Oil Shock and the World Economy* Hoboken: John Wiley and Sons.

Stovall, Sam. 2009. *The Seven Rules of Wall Street: Crash-Tested Investment Strategies That Beat the Market.* New York: McGraw Hill.

Wisdom, Gabriel. 2009. *Wisdom on Value Investing: How to Profit on Fallen Angels.* Hoboken: John Wiley and Sons.

Notes

CHAPTER 2

1. http://www.brainyquote.com/quotes/authors/w/warren_buffett.html
2. http://www.brainyquote.com/quotes/authors/j/john_maynard_keynes.html
3. Tergesen, Ann and Kim, Jane J., "Advisers Ditch Buy and Hold for New Tactics," Wall Street Journal Digital Network, April 29, 2009.

CHAPTER 3

1. http://www.brainyquote.com/quotes/authors/w/warren_buffett.html
2. Rozeff, Michael, "Lump Sum Investing versus Dollar Cost Averaging: Those Who Hesitate, Lose" *Journal of Portfolio Management*, Winter, 1994, pp. 45–50, http://www.altruistfa.com/readingroomarticles.htm
3. Stovall, Sam, *The Seven Rules of Wall Street: Crash Tested Investment Strategies That Beat the Market*, New York: McGraw Hill, 2009.

CHAPTER 4

1. Morningstar Reports U.S. Mutual Fund and ETF Asset Flows Through January 2010 http://www.prnewswire.com/news-releases/morningstar-reports-us-mutual-fund-and-etf-asset-flows-through-january-2010-84224032.html
2. Getting Personal: World-Wide ETF Assets Hit $1 Trillion. http://online.wsj.com/article/BT-CO-20100114-705467.html

CHAPTER 5

1. www.proshares.com
2. http://www.brainyquote.com/quotes/authors/w/warren_buffett.html

CHAPTER 14

1. http://www.brainyquote.com/quotes/authors/w/warren_buffett.html
2. Sun Tzu, *The Art of War*, Special Edition, English Translation and Commentary by Lionel Gates, Special Edition, El Paso Norte Press, March 2005.
3. Tich Nhat Hanh, *The Heart of the Buddha's Teaching*, Broadway Books, a division of Random House, 1999, pp. 51–113.

CHAPTER 17

1. McKinsey Global Institute, "Accounting for the Cost of U.S. Health Care: A New Look at Why Americans Spend More." June 2009, McKinsey Global Institute, McKinsey & Co., www.mckinsey.com/mgi

CHAPTER 18

1. Kurzweil, Raymond, "The Law of Accelerating Returns," March 7, 2001, KurzweilAI.net.

CHAPTER 19

1. http://www.brainyquote.com/quotes/authors/w/warren_buffett.html

About the Author

J ohn Nyaradi is Publisher of *Wall Street Sector Selector* (www.wall-street-sector-selector.com), an online newsletter specializing in sector rotation trading techniques and exchange traded funds. He is also President of Ridgeline Media Group, LLC and publishes a financial blog, *Wall Street Sector Selector: Professional ETF Trading*. Nyaradi's articles on investing have appeared in major online financial publications, including *Dow Jones Market Watch, Trading Markets, The Money Show, Yahoo Finance, InvestorsInsight, Fidelity.com, Seeking Alpha, ETF Daily News, iStockAnalyst,* and many others. He has also appeared as a guest on The Business Talk Radio Network.

Index

IBM, 190, 191
iMoney: Profitable Exchange Traded Fund Strategies for Every Investor, 220
India:
  as a potential super sector, 210, 216, 219
  technology and, 188
Indicators:
  adherence to, 157–158
  See also specific type
Individual Retirement Accounts, ETFs and, 37
Industrial Revolution, 173
Industrials sector, 49
  changes in, 50
  volatility and, 61
Inflation:
  asset allocation and risk of, 22
  buy and hold investors, 11
  sector rotation and, 52
Information, volatility and speed of, 57
Inger, Gene, 214–216
IngerLetter.com, 214
Insurance, investing in, 206
Intel, 190
Interest rates:
  exposure and asset allocation, 22
  financials as a super sector, 197
International Monetary Fund, Asia as a super sector, 171
Internet. *See* Technology, as a super sector
Internetworldstats.com, 188
Interstate Highway System, 189
Investing for a Lifetime, 228
Investor's Business Daily, 228
iPhones, 191
Iran, energy and, 176
Iraq:
  energy and, 176
  future of U.S. economy and, 207
Iron ore, 171
iShares FTSE/Xinhua China 25 Index (FXI), 37, 57, 59

iShares MSCI Emerging Markets Index (EEM):
  DBA and, 125, 126
  ETFs and, 35
    regional and broad based international ETFs, 37
  Point and Figure Charts
    Bullish Price Objective, 118, 119
    on buy signals, 115
    positive trend, 117
  Relative Strength, 108–109, 121, 122, 123
  SLV and, 127
Shares Russell 2000 (IWM), 35
iShares Silver Trust:
  money management stops and, 134
  point and figure trend lines, 140
  position size, 145–146
  Relative Strength, 109, 110
  setting stop loss, 143
  support levels, 137
  support and resistance trend lines, 139
  volatility-based stops, 136

Japan:
  buy and hold investors, impact of, 12
  energy and, 177
  technology and, 188
  as a U.S. creditor, 171
JDS Uniphase, 24
Jobs, Steve, 187
Journal of Behavioral Finance, 230
JP Morgan Chase and Co., 194

Kangas, Paul, 228
Keltner Channels, 208
Kenos Circle, 207
Kiplinger's Personal Finance, 228
Kissinger, Henry, 178
Korea, South:
  economy, 171
  as a super sector, 216
  technology and, 188
  as a U.S. creditor, 171
  See also Asia, as a super sector